"A refreshing, clearly-written, thought-provoking, truly enjoyable book that will help overcome many misconceptions and deepen people's faith and joy in God each day."
> **Wayne Grudem,** Research Professor of Bible and Theology, Phoenix Seminary

"Calvinism gets a lot of bad press because of its joyless believers. Yet joyless Calvinism is an oxymoron. Forster has helped reframe this beautiful understanding of God in the Scriptures in a way that is attractive and compelling."
> **Darrin Patrick,** Lead Pastor, The Journey, St. Louis, Missouri; author, *For the City* and *Church Planter*

"Forster pulls few punches with his critiques both for Calvinists and also their opponents—this vigor is what makes this exploration of joyous Calvinism so welcome and so challenging."
> **Collin Hansen,** Editorial Director, The Gospel Coalition; author, *Young, Restless, Reformed*

"Concerned that some of the negative press which Calvinism receives is actually provoked by Calvinists themselves, Forster here offers a refreshing restatement of the Reformed faith. In the tradition of the personal confidence and joy one finds in the Heidelberg Catechism, he presents an account of the Reformed understanding of salvation that is accessible, reliable, and delightful. A super book to read for oneself or to give to Christian friends who may never have understood the joy that lies at the heart of Calvinism."
> **Carl R. Trueman,** Paul Woolley Professor of Church History, Westminster Theological Seminary, Pennsylvania

"Calvinism has been the target of countless caricatures, but none so misguided as the notion that it is the enemy of joy. Forster insists rightly that Calvinism is 'drenched with joy,' and has done a masterful job of accounting for the beauty and delight intrinsic to biblical Calvinism. I pray this book gets a wide reading."
> **Sam Storms,** Senior Pastor, Bridgeway Church, Oklahoma City, Oklahoma; author, *The Hope of Glory*

"Forster does a wonderful, twofold service for God's people in this book—he retrieves Calvinism from a portrayal as a dark and distasteful version of Christianity and, instead, presents it as an attractive and beautiful expression of biblical religion. Forster speaks with deep wisdom rooted not only in a well-informed theology, but also from his own experience as he wrestled with the sufferings of life and ultimately found comfort in the God who is profoundly merciful and sovereign in Christ. I highly recommend this book for all who seek godly encouragement and joy in the midst of life's trials."

David VanDrunen, Robert B. Strimple Professor of Systematic Theology and Christian Ethics, Westminster Seminary California; author, *Bioethics and the Christian Life*

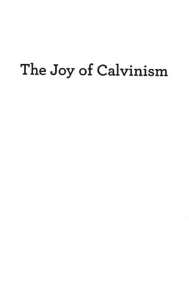

The Joy of Calvinism

the

JOY

of

CALVINISM

Knowing God's Personal, Unconditional,
Irresistible, Unbreakable Love

GREG FORSTER

∷ CROSSWAY

WHEATON, ILLINOIS

The Joy of Calvinism: Knowing God's Personal,
Unconditional, Irresistible, Unbreakable Love

Copyright © 2012 by Greg Forster

Published by Crossway
1300 Crescent Street
Wheaton, Illinois 60187

Cover design: Josh Dennis

Cover illustrator: Darren Booth / darrenbooth.com

First printing 2012

Printed in the United States of America

Trade paperback ISBN: 978-1-4335-2834-7
PDF ISBN: 978-1-4335-2835-4
Mobipocket ISBN: 978-1-4335-2836-1
ePub ISBN: 978-1-4335-2837-8

Library of Congress Cataloging-in-Publication Data
The joy of Calvinism : knowing God's personal, unconditional, irresistible, unbreakable love / Greg Forster.
    p. cm.
Includes bibliographical references and index.
ISBN 978-1-4335-2834-7 (tp)
    1. Calvinism. 2. God (Christianity)—Love. 3. Theology, Doctrinal.
4. Salvation—Christianity. 5. Joy—Religious aspects—Calvinists.
6. Christian life. I. Title.
BX9422.3.F67   2012
230'.42—dc23   2011035957

Crossway is a publishing ministry of Good News Publishers.

VP		22	21	20	19	18	17	16	15	14	13	12
15	14	13	12	11	10	9	8	7	6	5	4	3	2	1

For Larry Wilson, my father in Christ

Though you have countless guides in Christ,
you do not have many fathers.
For I became your father in Christ Jesus
through the gospel. I urge you, then,
be imitators of me. (1 Cor. 4:15–16)

Contents

Acknowledgments 11

Introduction: Rejoice . . . Always? 13

Detour: Five Points about Calvinism 29

1 God Loves You Personally 47
  When Jesus died and rose again, he saved you.

2 God Loves You Unconditionally 69
  Nothing is more important to your heavenly Father than saving you.

3 God Loves You Irresistibly 91
  The "new birth" in the Holy Spirit is a radical, supernatural transformation.

4 God Loves You Unbreakably 121
  You can do all things, persevere through all trials, and rejoice in all circumstances.

Conclusion: The Joy of Calvinism 145

Appendix: Questions and Answers 155

Notes 197

General Index 201

Scripture Index 203

Acknowledgments

My deepest thanks go out to Crossway and my editor Allan Fisher for giving me the extraordinary opportunity to offer you this book, and for helping me to make it the book that it is.

Frank Marsh and Dan Kelly read the entire manuscript and gave me detailed feedback, which greatly improved the book. I also received invaluable ideas, advice, assistance, feedback, and encouragement from Larry Wilson, Glenn Moots, Caroline Stack, Kenneth Stewart, Jim Rahn, Ryan Olson, Stephen Grabill, Jordan Ballor, Wayne Grudem, and anonymous reviewers at Crossway.

Almost the entirety of this book was written away from home. I was the beneficiary of generous hospitality from my coworker Ryan Olson and his family, and on another occasion from Caroline Stack.

As always, everything I do is made possible only by the unflagging encouragement and colabor of my wife, Beth. And this is the first book I've written for which my daughter, Anya, was old enough to add her own words of support and encouragement. When I emerged from my office and told her that I only had a tiny bit of work left and the manuscript I was working on would be finished, her response was: "So go back and do it!" Truly, the Lord has brought forth his Word from the mouths of little children.

Above all, I give thanks to the Lord. "This is the message we have heard from him and proclaim to you, that God is light, and in him is no darkness at all" (1 John 1:5).

Introduction

Rejoice . . . Always?

The Bible commands us to rejoice all the time. God says that if there is even a tiny fraction of a split second when we're not rejoicing, that's disobedience. The command is shocking, bewildering, and—to be blunt—deeply offensive. It is impossible. It is as if God demanded that I lift a house over my head and threatened me with severe discipline if I failed.

We are, of course, prepared to accept some level of accountability for our emotions. We understand that we are corrupt sinners whose emotions are badly out of line with God's standards. We love the wrong things, hate the wrong things, are thrilled or sickened by the wrong things, get sad or angry when we shouldn't and don't get sad or angry when we should, and experience emotions like grudge holding and vengefulness that no one should ever experience at any time whatsoever. Getting our hearts cleaned up is going to be a long, hard slog. We know that. It's going to be painful, it's going to be humiliating, it's going to be death to self every day. If God were demanding that, we wouldn't exactly be jumping up and down with excitement, but we'd be ready to hear it.

But God is not demanding that. God does not say, "Get to work fixing your emotions so that you will eventually get into a state of mind, heart, and will, such that you can and do rejoice at all times." He simply orders us to rejoice at all times—right now, this moment—as though we had the power to do it at will, just like that.

This is really quite clear in the Bible. "Rejoice in the Lord always; again I will say, Rejoice" (Phil. 4:4). "Rejoice always, pray without ceasing, give thanks in all circumstances; for this is the will of God in Christ Jesus for you" (1 Thess. 5:16–18). For good measure, it even tells us to "rejoice in our sufferings" (Rom. 5:3).

What can it possibly mean?

I wrote this book because I believe Calvinism points to the answer. Obviously I'm not saying only Calvinists have joy. I'm saying that if you want to understand the command to rejoice at all times, and still more if you want to obey it, of all the places you might start looking for help with that problem, the best place to start is with Calvinism.

Failure to Communicate

It seems to me that Calvinists, myself included, have not been communicating well about our ideas. And we have tended to blame the audience for what are really our own failures in communicating.

Here's what I mean. Our little daughter, Anya, has difficulty with language, and this has made it a challenge for us to teach her about God. At one point, I got it into my head to try a new way of helping her understand what's going on during the worship service. Anya knew some things about God, but she didn't understand what church had to do with him. So I decided to try using the fundamental principle of the Calvinistic understanding of worship, which is that the worship service is not primarily something we do for God, that it's something God does for us. God is actively working in every part of the service; we participate, of course, but we are receiving much more than we are giving—we are far more passive than active.

So during each part of the service, I would tell Anya what God was doing. During the call to worship I would tell her, "God is saying hi to us!" During the sermon I would tell her, "God is telling us his Word!" During the benediction I would say, "God is blessing us!"

From all this, Anya learned exactly one thing: the pastor is God.

Needless to say, I changed my approach to communicating with Anya about God. I'm greatly relieved to report that we've cleared up this unfortunate misunderstanding, and Anya is making great progress learning about the Lord. Recently, she overheard a woman in a coffee shop misuse the name of Jesus as a swear word. Anya understood nothing about what she was hearing except the name Jesus, but when she heard that name, she immediately piped up and said in a loud voice, "Jesus loves me!" (The woman mumbled something about being more careful with what she said in front of children.) You can imagine what a relief it is for my wife and me to see that we're now successfully conveying these precious truths about God and Jesus to our daughter. Not to mention that she's already witnessing her faith!

It makes a big difference how you communicate your ideas. It's not just what you say; it's how you phrase and frame it. The difficulty I faced with Anya wasn't simply that she has trouble processing information. The bigger problem was on my end—I was presenting the information to her in a way that invited misunderstanding. When I changed the way I communicated, she was able to understand me.

We Calvinists need to do the same.

Beyond Formulas to Joy

In this book, I use "Calvinism" to mean the soteriology—the understanding of how sinners are saved—that has developed over time in the faith tradition that traces its history back through Calvin. The Calvinistic faith tradition is really much more than that, of course; it has a distinctive approach to pretty much everything. But our understanding of how sinners get saved is what most needs clarifying.

The world misunderstands what Calvinists believe about salvation. The misunderstanding is not just on the margins, but radical—almost as radical as Anya's misunderstanding about God. I think that's because we usually present what we believe in a way that invites misunderstanding.

Real Calvinism is all about joy. But for some time now, defenders of Calvinism have tended to communicate about it only in highly technical, formulaic, and (especially) negative terms. To take only the most obvious example, the notorious "five points of

Calvinism" are now virtually the only terms in which Calvinism is formulated. The five points that we now use didn't even exist until the twentieth century and weren't widely used until the second half of that century.[1] Even then, they used to be just one framework among many for talking about Calvinism. But today, these five vague phrases abbreviated by a clever acronym (TULIP) have come to be completely identified with Calvinism. If you tell people you want to defend Calvinism, you're saying you want to defend the five points. What else could "Calvinism" possibly mean? (If you're not familiar with the "five points" and want to know more about them, see the appendix, question 2.)

Bafflingly, this has happened even though many Calvinist writers seem to agree that the five points are a lousy way to describe Calvinism! The five points use highly technical and idiosyncratic terms that invite misunderstanding. And they're almost entirely negative; they tell you a lot about what Calvinists don't believe but very little about what Calvinists do believe. It sometimes feels like Calvinists first invoke the five points, then apologize for invoking the five points, and then explain how the five points don't really mean what they seem to mean and aren't really saying what they seem to be saying. This can't possibly be the best way to introduce people to what we believe.

What makes this especially puzzling is that Calvinists usually don't have this problem when they write about John Calvin the man, or other great heroes of faith within the Calvinist tradition, or just about anything else besides Calvinism itself. They will write with great eloquence about Calvin's passion for God and his pastor's heart for bringing God's Word and God's comfort to ordinary people, or about Augustine or John Newton, or the beauty and purity of the Reformed worship tradition, or the real spiritual presence of Christ in the Lord's Supper. But when the subject is Calvinism itself—the distinctive theology that provides the underlying basis for all the other beautiful Calvinistic things they write so eloquently about—they suddenly shift gears and retreat to formulas and technicalities.

The trouble is that people outside the Calvinistic tradition only hear the formulas and technicalities. They don't hear what we say "within" Calvinism; they only hear what we say *about* Calvinism. So while Calvinists produce reams and reams of positive, spontaneous, and devotional religious writings, the outside world never knows. If it hears our devotional voices at all, it never associates that devotion with our Calvinism; it thinks we're pious in spite of our Calvinism, not because of it. "Calvinism" to the outside world means only the formulas, technicalities, and negations.

As a result, the substantial reality of Calvinistic religion, the affirmative faith from which it draws all its energy and vitality and joy, is almost completely unknown to the outside world. Even most of the people who worship in Calvinistic churches, and are thus nominally "Calvinists," don't understand what really makes Calvinistic religion such a precious treasure. Because we don't communicate clearly, our own congregants have a very inadequate grasp of what lies at the heart of Calvinism. As a result, they're robbed—in whole or in part—of the everyday experience of devotional joy that a robust and well-formed Calvinistic piety always produces, and in which, as Calvinists, they ought to be living.

What would happen if we talked about other theological topics, such as the divinity of Christ, the way we usually talk about Calvinism?[2] Consider two different historic confessions of the divinity of Christ, both of which play essential roles in Christian theology and history. First, consider Thomas, falling to his knees (or so we picture him) before the resurrected Christ, crying out in that perfect combination of shock, joy, love, awe, repentance, self-abasement, and holy terror, "My Lord and my God!"(John 20:28). Now compare that confession with the early medieval priests rhythmically chanting the metered Latin of the Athanasian Creed: "Although he is God and man, yet he is not two, but one Christ; one, not by conversion of the Godhead into flesh, but by assumption of the manhood into God; one altogether, not by confusion of essence, but by unity of person; for as the reasonable soul and flesh is one man, so God and man is one Christ."

There is no question that the latter sort of confession—formalistic, technical, and negative—is indispensable in keeping the church's confession pure from faith-destroying errors. Without the Athanasian Creed and other formulations like it, Christianity could not possibly have survived the relentless assaults against the doctrines of the Trinity and the Incarnation in its first five centuries. You and I would not be Christians today.

Yet there would have been nothing to protect—no Christianity for the Athanasian Creed to keep pure in the first place—if not for the sort of confession we get from Thomas. Here, and only here, we have the spontaneous voice of living Christian faith, expressing what the believer really experiences in the presence of the living Christ. True, this faith could not have survived if it had not been protected by the shield of technical theology, but that shield was forged only to protect and nurture spontaneous, affirmative faith. It has no other legitimate function. An "Athanasius confession" without a "Thomas confession" is just as dead, empty, and useless as a suit of armor without a knight inside. Athanasius himself would have been the first to insist on this!

Thomas faith—and only Thomas faith—gives Christianity all its spiritual power. How many doubters would come to accept the divinity of Christ if the only thing they ever heard about it was the Athanasian Creed?

That's about where we are right now in talking to the world about Calvinism. We're rhythmically chanting our technical formulas, not only in the times and places where technical formulas are properly called for, but all the time. Athanasius could fall down on his knees with Thomas and say, "My Lord and my God!" We need to remember how to fall down on our knees and say, with Peter:

> Blessed be the God and Father of our Lord Jesus Christ! According to his great mercy, he has caused us to be born again to a living hope

through the resurrection of Jesus Christ from the dead, to an inheritance that is imperishable, undefiled, and unfading, kept in heaven for you, who by God's power are being guarded through faith for a salvation ready to be revealed in the last time. In this you rejoice, though now for a little while, if necessary, you have been grieved by various trials, so that the tested genuineness of your faith—more precious than gold that perishes though it is tested by fire—may be found to result in praise and glory and honor at the revelation of Jesus Christ. (1 Peter 1:3–7)

We say things like this often enough; it's time we showed people that this is really what Calvinism is all about.

Other Christians say the same things, of course—they're in Scripture, after all! But they miss, or ignore, or explain away the full meaning. That's why it's so important to point the way to the fullness of joy and power and peace that can only be had by grasping that full meaning firmly and holding on tight. Being a Calvinist means living in the fullness of joy that Peter expresses in this passage, by embracing its full meaning and all the implications of that meaning for doctrine, piety, and life. Defending Calvinism means defending that fullness of joy by defending that full meaning.

What Calvinism Tastes Like

There are a million books out there claiming that "everything you know about" some subject "is wrong." This is another one. But in this case it's really justified. The absence of affirmative and spontaneously devotional expression of Calvinistic theology has left a gaping hole in the public understanding of what Calvinism is.

Put simply, the rest of the world has no idea what it's *like* to be a Calvinist. It's like trying to describe Italian food by making a list of all the things it doesn't taste like. When you get to the end of the list, you won't really know more about the taste of Italian food than you did when you started.

And that's not the worst of it. When we don't show people what Calvinistic religion is really like, they form impressions of it based on other sources. The law that "nature abhors a vacuum" applies to the human mind and spirit as much as to physical nature.

If you're an average American Christian from a non-Calvinist background, the (sort of) accurate information you receive about Calvinists is probably limited to the following: Calvinists don't think people have any natural ability to repent and trust Christ. They don't think people have ultimate control over their final destinies. They don't think Jesus died and rose again to atone for the sins of all humanity. They don't think God allows us to choose whether to follow him. And they think "once saved, always saved." That's it. Then, alongside this (sort of) accurate information, you've probably also heard that Calvinists think we don't have free will (i.e., human beings are not responsible moral agents but are puppets under the control of exterior forces), that unbelievers are as evil as they can possibly be, and that God doesn't love unbelievers. You may have been told that Jonathan Edwards—the greatest American exponent of Calvinism and a figure of titanic importance to the history of the Calvinist tradition—described the work of the Holy Spirit in the hearts of believers as "holy rape."

Based on this information, what would it be natural for you to conclude about Calvinists? What would you naturally expect was the motivation for their belief in Calvinism, and what would you think their devotional lives were like? At best, you would think Calvinism was theological oversystematization gone horribly haywire—like those atheist philosophers who firmly insist that human beings cannot think and are not conscious because that's what their materialistic assumptions imply, and they're prepared to defend their assumptions in the teeth of all absurdity. At worst, you would think Calvinism was a manifestation of thoroughly demonic self-righteousness and presumption.

And all of that is before the more irresponsible opponents of Calvinism have even opened their mouths. It's no wonder they find a receptive audience when they falsely attribute to us all sorts of absurd and wicked beliefs and spin their tales about Calvin the bloodthirsty tyrant, who delighted in nothing but endless torture and slaughter of heretics. All of that propaganda is naturally plausible to the millions of American Christians who know nothing about Calvinism except its technical formulas.

Renewing Our Minds—Spiritually

This book is mostly about our daily walk with God—all the triumphs and failures, the death to self, and the invitations to joy that make up the Christian life as we really live it. But this book also deals with something that is called, in the jargon of academia, "systematic theology." In seminaries, systematic theology is carefully distinguished from Bible scholarship. Systematic theology is the attempt to express the integrated, coherent testimony of all Scripture taken together, while Bible scholarship is the study of individual Bible texts.

Many people don't accept the legitimacy of systematic theology. They want the text of the Bible and nothing else. If you step away from the texts of Scripture, they think you must have also stepped away from the teachings of Scripture.

But you cannot really go without systematic theology, and in fact there is no one who does. Those who claim that their theology is "the Bible and only the Bible" have simply taken their systematic theology, whatever it may be, and relabeled it as "the Bible." I don't see how you can be a Christian if you don't have an answer to the question "What do you think the Bible teaches?" Your answer, whatever it is, is your systematic theology.

Bible scholarship and systematic theology must cooperate closely in order for either of them to be of any use. Systematic theology must be grounded in the final authority of the Bible, so it must be informed by what individual Scripture texts teach us. And our reading of any individual Bible passage must, in turn, be informed by the testimony of the rest of Scripture taken together.

Nonetheless, it is not usually possible to do both at the same time. At any rate I certainly can't, since I'm not a trained scholar in either field! So you should not expect to find detailed expositions or examinations of specific Scripture passages in this book. I do quote some passages of Scripture to support some of my arguments, but if you're looking for extensive interaction with the text, you won't find it here. Other authors—who are real Bible scholars—have already written an endless series of books going over particular texts to debate whether they teach, or are consistent with, Calvinism.

My goal is different but equally important. I want to tell you what Calvinism says, especially what it says about your everyday walk with God and the purpose of the Christian life, and how you can have the joy of God even in spite of whatever trials and suffering the Lord has called you to endure. I think most people today are either ignorant or badly mistaken about what Calvinism really is, especially when it comes to these practical applications in everyday life. And you can't very well examine Scripture to find out whether it teaches, or is consistent with, Calvinism until you know what Calvinism really is. Once you understand that, then you can go see whether or not it is the coherent teaching that emerges from the integrated witness of Scripture. My goal is not to examine Scripture extensively but to put you in a position to do so.

Taking Our Ignorance Seriously
I've mentioned that some people don't accept systematic theology. One reason for this is a problem that we will be encountering throughout this book. God is infinite (unlimited) in many ways— infinitely powerful, infinitely good, infinitely knowing, infinitely wise, infinitely present, and so on. We, on the other hand, are finite (limited) in every way. We are not infinitely anything.

That means we can never totally understand anything about God. His infinite reality can't fit into our finite understandings. Theologians refer to this as the "incomprehensibility" of God. This doesn't mean we can't understand anything about God. Obviously we can. It means we can't understand everything about God. And we must take our ignorance seriously.

One of the most important reasons people reject systematic

theology is that they want to take seriously our ignorance about God. That is an important concern. But, in fact, God has made our minds in such a way that we cannot make practical use of any knowledge—including the knowledge he gives us about himself—unless we systematize it. Whether we're talking about theology or science or literature or child rearing or figuring out where I left my car keys, we have to take the available data and organize them into a coherent whole from which we can draw conclusions.

The danger is that we will forget to take our ignorance seriously. And one of the interesting things about theological disputes—especially the dispute between Calvinism and its rivals—is that each side thinks the other side goes wrong partly by not taking our ignorance seriously. Calvinists think that the other traditions assume they know more about God than they really know. Non-Calvinists think the same thing about Calvinists.

The starting point for a serious conversation is to acknowledge that the basic teachings of Christianity are deeply mysterious. We believe them because God tells us about them and we trust God, not because we understand them. Free will and providence are mysterious. We are, somehow, in control of our own actions such that we are responsible for them (Ezekiel 18). Yet this does not exclude God's being in control of everything that occurs, down to the smallest events (Matt. 10:29–31) and including our actions (Gen. 50:20; Rom. 9:19–23; 1 Thess. 5:9; 1 Pet. 2:8). God planned everything that would ever happen before he created the world, yet we are in control of our actions moment by moment.

Original sin is mysterious. We are, somehow, born already guilty and corrupt (Romans 5). We are guilty of sin before we have ever committed a single sin. We are predisposed to sin before we have had any experiences to form our predispositions. And somehow both of these realities are consistent with our free will.

Atonement is mysterious. We are guilty and God never acquits the guilty (Ex. 34:7; Num. 14:18; Nah. 1:3). Jesus is righteous and God never convicts the righteous (Gen. 18:27–33). Yet, somehow,

God changes our statuses so that we become righteous and Jesus becomes guilty on the cross (2 Cor. 5:21; 1 Pet. 2:24). Talk about mystery!

We don't even need to bring in God to find mystery. The human mind, heart, and will are deeply mysterious simply considered in themselves. Even the tiniest things about us are completely inexplicable. How can I forget what something looks like, then recognize it the next time I see it? If I forgot what it looks like, why do I recognize it? There's no end to the unanswerable questions we can ask about ourselves. Attempts to wrestle with these questions usually produce little more than confusion, question begging, circular reasoning, and finally (if people are honest enough) confessions of ignorance. In this book, I will not attempt to explain or investigate these mysteries. Rather, I want to take for granted their mysteriousness and ask what we can know about God in that context based on what God has told us about himself.

One final word on this topic: although we must take our ignorance seriously, we must also take seriously our knowledge. Both the knowledge we already possess and our capacity for learning more come from God, and he demands that we make good use of them.

Theology may correct people if they have incorrect ideas, but it may not simply tell people to forget everything they already think and substitute some new body of knowledge instead. That is not how God himself speaks to us in the Bible. God does not present an argument that he exists or that there is such a thing as right and wrong. He assumes you already know, and it's a safe assumption because he gave you that knowledge when he made you (Romans 1–2). He then corrects the various errors and perversions you have laid on top of this knowledge, and he does it precisely by pointing to the things you already know and demanding that you be faithful to them.

In other words, we can never say that everything we think is true, God says is false, and that everything we think is good, God says is bad. Not *everything*. If we said that, we'd be denying the image of God in ourselves. And—more important for the purposes of this book—we'd be denying that we can ever possibly know anything about what God says is true and good. We'd be admitting that we don't worship God for the right reasons.

If we discover—really discover, as opposed to just saying it—that something we thought was true about God is actually false, or that something we thought was good is actually bad, it will be because we see a deeper truth or a deeper goodness that we really knew about all along but had forgotten or twisted out of shape. We must be ready to reexamine all our beliefs in light of Scripture because we're finite and sinful, and so we require correction from our Lord. But we don't need to be worried that God's truth and goodness are fundamentally different, all the way down, from our truth and goodness. They can't be. We're made in his image.

Brothers and Sisters After All

As we turn to the broader conversation, let me open with a provocative observation and an urgent warning. The provocative observation is that Calvinism does not really confess anything that isn't also confessed by all the other major Christian theological traditions—not ultimately, not at its heart. All the major traditions confess the same doctrines that are central to Calvinism: original sin, the sovereignty of God, substitutionary atonement, supernatural regeneration, and so forth. What makes Calvinism Calvinism is not so much that it has something that other traditions lack, but that it preserves these doctrinal commitments more purely and follows them more consistently than other traditions do. It does so not by adding anything to them but by striving to reject and expel a foreign element—the attribution of God's supernatural works to human or other natural causes.

The impulse to attribute God's saving work to humanity or nature has existed, to a greater or lesser degree, in all parts of the church at all times. The impulse is so strong that even the churches planted by the apostles themselves seem to have been constantly falling back into it—and not centuries later, but while the apostles were still living. In fact, the special purpose for which Jesus appointed the apostles was not to plant churches (lots of people did that) but to correct churches when they went off the rails in precisely this way. In the apostolic Epistles, as in the Hebrew prophets before them, we hear the battle trumpets of the great spiritual war to expel this foreign element from our hearts, minds, and lives. This war is almost by definition the struggle of the church militant in every age.

For those of us who are Calvinists, Calvinism is just our name for this war. I don't mean that we're the only ones who fight the war. All branches of the church agree, in principle, that we must fight it; we agree, in principle, that it is God who works salvation. But those of us who are Calvinists believe that the rest of the church has not gone far enough in prosecuting the war. Many of the teachings that the rest of the church believes to be truth, we believe to be a series of compromises in which the truth is mixed together with the very error that we are all agreed, in principle, must be rejected.

This, of course, explains why Calvinists tend to lapse into technical formulas of negation so often when they talk about Calvinism. To some extent, we have to do so; we must negate the attribution of God's supernatural work to human and natural causes. The problem is that we Calvinists have become so uniformly negative that people no longer recognize that Calvinists share the same fundamental doctrinal commitments as non-Calvinists—that our negations are intended to guard the same things everybody else wants to guard. We just disagree about how to guard them.

This view also provides an explanation for a strange fact—a fact that people find so surprising and incredible that they often don't believe it even when they see it with their own eyes. I mean the fact that Calvinistic religion is so drenched with joy. Everyone expects Calvinists to be sour and flat souled, and when they discover just how false this is (if they do ever allow themselves to be sufficiently exposed to Calvinism that they discover it), they respond with puzzlement and even with disbelief. But there's no mystery about it. Without Calvinism, Christian religion filters God through a series of spurious claims attributing God's direct and supernatural works to ourselves, or the church, or nature generally. With Calvinism, we get God pure and unfiltered. And, if you will forgive what may be a scandalous metaphor: the purer the drug, the more potent the high.

The adherents of other traditions, of course, see things differently. I don't want to offend my brothers and sisters in Christ, but I do want to serve them by telling them what I think—just as I always rejoice to hear them tell me what they think. And there is a very weighty matter for mutual celebration here. It turns out we're not as different as we thought. It turns out the heart and soul of Calvinism can be expressed as nothing more than a call to be fully faithful to the light, as God gives us ability to see the light, of the same truths that other Christians also confess. It turns out we're all striving to preserve the same truth. *It turns out we really are brothers and sisters after all.*

Warning against Presumption
Now for the urgent warning. Throughout this book I speak of the promises of salvation with reference to "you"—as in, "when Jesus died and rose again, he saved you"—on the assumption that you, the reader, possess those promises. If you have genuinely repented from sin, trusted Christ alone as your Savior and Lord, and embarked upon a life of active discipleship through obedience and service to others, you do. If not, you don't.

I beg you, examine your life to know whether you have truly done so. I speak as someone who once had a false assurance of salvation. I know firsthand how easy it is for a self-righteous man to preserve his delusional opinion of his own goodness and his demonic presumption upon God's grace. The key method of self-deception about your salvation is to avoid self-examination about the state of your life. The biblical basis of assurance is to test the fruits of your faith in your life by God's standards; that's what the famous passage in 2 Peter 1:1–11 and the whole book of 1 John are all about. Don't delay—lay your life out on the examining table this day, this hour, this moment. And whatever you find, evaluate it by God's standards and offer it to him, knowing that "if we confess our sins, he is faithful and just to forgive us our sins and to cleanse us from all unrighteousness" (1 John 1:9).

Detour

Five Points about Calvinism

In the introduction, I said that Calvinism is radically misunderstood by most people in our day. I expect that at that point, my readers divided into two groups. One group really wants to hear me make the case to support that assertion, either because they disagree with it or because they're undecided and are interested in hearing my argument. The other group doesn't need to hear me make the case on this, either because they already agree with me or because they're not interested in the issue—they picked up this book to hear about the joy of Calvinism, not an argument over whether Calvinism is misunderstood. This section is a detour for the benefit of the first group. Members of the second group may feel free to skip it entirely.

To try to convince you of just how drastically Calvinism has been miscommunicated and misunderstood, let me offer my own five points about Calvinism. I'm willing to bet that they'll challenge most people's conception of Calvinism in a pretty fundamental way. These points challenge five common myths about Calvinism. I think these myths are the main reason people don't hear what Calvinism really has to say.

To support my five points, I need to refer to an objective standard of what Calvinists believe. I want you to know that when I say Calvinists believe this or that, I'm not just making things up as I go. To confirm that I'm accurately representing Calvinism, I use the Westminster Confession of Faith as a standard of reference.[1] Of course, there's no authoritative or mandatory doctrinal statement that all Calvinists without exception unconditionally accept.

But we need to use something as a reference, and the Westminster Confession is the overwhelmingly predominant confessional statement of Calvinist theology in the English-speaking world. This is the statement that most confessionally Calvinist church bodies require their clergy to affirm. That's more than enough for my purposes. If I want to prove that "Calvinism doesn't say *x*," pointing out that the Westminster Confession says "*x* is false" is pretty much a slam dunk.

1. Calvinism does not deny that we have free will.

The Westminster Confession has a whole chapter called "Of Free Will." Here is the first section of that chapter, in its entirety:

> God hath endued the will of man with that natural liberty, that it is neither forced, nor, by any absolute necessity of nature, determined to good, or evil. (WCF 9.1)

You can't get much clearer than that.

Earlier in the Confession there's a chapter on God's providential guiding of his creation. Again in the very first section, the authors make a point of affirming free will:

> God, from all eternity, did, by the most wise and holy counsel of his own will, freely, and unchangeably ordain whatsoever comes to pass: yet so, as thereby neither is God the author of sin, nor is violence offered to the will of the creatures; nor is the liberty or contingency of second causes taken away, but rather established. (WCF 3.1)

In case you're wondering, when the Confession refers to "second causes," human will is one of the things included in that category. But affirming the liberty of "second causes" in general wasn't enough for the Confession's authors. They went out of their way to specifically insist that in God's providential control of events there is no "violence offered to the will of the creatures."[2]

Of course, there is much more to be said about these issues, and this isn't the place to get into all the technicalities. The important point for our purposes here is that Calvinism clearly and unambiguously insists that we have free will. (For more about these issues, see the appendix, questions 5 and 6.)

If so, why do so many people think Calvinism denies free will? Where did that idea come from?

Today, the phrase "free will" refers to moral responsibility. When we say people have free will, we mean that they are not just puppets of exterior natural forces such as their heredity and environment; they are in control of their own choices and are morally responsible for them. In our language, the opposite of "free will" is "determined will"—a will whose actions are naturally determined by things outside itself.

But in the sixteenth century, at the very beginning of the Reformation, one of the key debates was over "free will" in a completely different sense. The question then was whether the will is, by nature, enslaved by sin and in captivity to Satan. In this context, the opposite of "free" is not "determined" but "enslaved." Believing in "free will" meant believing that human beings are not born as slaves of Satan. Denying "free will" meant believing that they are.

Erasmus, one of Luther's most perceptive and influential critics, solidified this use of the term "free will" in his book *The Freedom of the Will*. Erasmus argued that the key issue between Luther and Rome was whether we are born as slaves of Satan or born free to choose whether to serve God or Satan. Luther strongly agreed that this was, indeed, the key issue; he praised Erasmus for being the only person on Rome's side smart enough to grasp this. When Luther wrote a book in reply to Erasmus's *The Freedom of the Will*, he entitled it *The Slavery of the Will*. Many others on both sides picked up this theme—including Calvin, who took the same position as Luther. Calvin entitled his own book on the subject *The Slavery and Liberation of the Will*. Denying "free will" (in this particular sense) was one of the earliest defining positions of both Lutheran and Calvinistic theology. It was an essential element of the Protestant view.

In these debates, nobody was questioning that the will is "free" in the sense of self-controlled and morally responsible, as opposed to being determined by exterior forces. Everyone agreed that people have "free will" in this sense, but people didn't call it "free will" because that phrase had a different meaning for them. Calvin even called the slavery of the will to Satan "voluntary slavery." Fallen man is a slave of Satan precisely because, when given a choice, he always chooses to love sin more than God. It is his own voluntary choice (his exercise of "free will" in our modern sense) that keeps him a slave to Satan (thus lacking "free will" in the sixteenth-century sense).

Moreover, at one point in the *Institutes of the Christian Religion*, his theological masterwork, Calvin actually turns aside from a diatribe against "free will" to make this very point. He notes that the phrase "free will" could also be used to refer to a morally responsible will that is not naturally determined by forces such as heredity and environment, and he says if "free will" means that, then he agrees we have "free will." But, he goes on to argue, that's not what most people (at least in his time and place) would understand that phrase to mean, so it would be misleading for him to use it that way.[3]

Our problem is that people who study the sixteenth-century debates often carry its phrases into the discussions and debates of our own time without adjusting for the change in meaning. Of course it's natural and right for scholarly study of these theological issues to be shaped by the great books that were written during the sixteenth-century Reformation debate. However, we often don't consider carefully enough how those books continue to shape our language—especially when we talk to audiences made up of people who don't read five-hundred-year-old books on a regular basis. And the phrase "free will" today has a radically different meaning from the one it took on in the context of the sixteenth-century Reformation debate.

Calvin wrote that he used the term "free will" the way he did because he didn't want to create misunderstanding. But when we use it that same way today, misunderstanding is exactly what we create. We would do better to emulate Calvin in his desire to avoid misunderstanding rather than in his particular lexicographical choices.

2. Calvinism does not say we are saved against our wills.

This point is just another application of the general truth that Calvinism strongly affirms the free will of all people. Just as God's providential control of all events does not, on the Calvinist view, negate the free will of human beings in general, the particular work of the Holy Spirit in bringing believers to faith doesn't negate the free will of those individuals.

In fact, the parallel between the two cases goes much deeper. God's providential control of all events, far from negating the freedom of our wills, is actually the source of that freedom. It is God's eternal decree that our wills be free, so his providential control sustains our freedom. Similarly, the saving work of the Spirit preserves the freedom of our wills rather than negating it.

Section 10.1 of the Westminster Confession, which describes the work of the Holy Spirit in converting sinners, insists that when the Spirit is "drawing them to Jesus Christ" they "come most freely." As we saw above with the free will of the whole human race, so here with the free will of God's people during their regeneration and conversion—the Confession goes out of its way to affirm the free will of human beings. Just as God the Creator gives all people free will in their original nature, so God the Savior preserves the free will of his children as he gives them a new nature.

Again, there is much more to be said, and this is not the place for technical discussion. The important point is that you can't be a Calvinist, according to the Confession, unless you affirm free will. (See the appendix, question 5.)

In fact, the work of the Spirit enlarges our freedom. Who is more free, the inquisitive and learned man or the contented ignoramus? Who is more free, the sober and self-controlled man or the addict? Who is more free, the man with natural and well-ordered desires or the pervert? In one important sense, they are all equally free.

That is, they are all free to act within the bounds of their capacities and powers, and they are all fully responsible for their actions. And yet, those whose capacities and powers give them a wider scope to exercise their freedom are, in another important sense, freer. The addict is free, but the sober man is (in one sense) freer. The addict can freely struggle to overcome his addiction or freely wallow in it, but the sober man is free to do many other things—such as receiving the ordinary enjoyment that God intended us to get from moderate drinking, or having relationships that aren't disrupted by the struggle with drunkenness—that the addict isn't free to do because of his addiction.

It's the same, but on a much more profound level, with the work of the Spirit. The natural human life is dominated by ignorance, impotence, frustration, compulsion, self-obsession, solipsism, disappointment, and (at best) resignation. The Christ life that the Spirit puts into us lives into ever more abundant knowledge, power, self-control, self-givingness, pleasure, contentment, and joy. In one sense, we are as free as we ever were—free to act within the life we have. But in another sense, who would not agree that the freedom to live as a slave is a lesser freedom than the freedom to live as a god (Ps. 82:6, John 10:34–36)?

It's true that, on the Calvinistic view, the Holy Spirit does not ask our permission before working this change in our hearts. But the change that he works is a change that makes us more free, not less. Here is yet another parallel to the work of creation—we all agree that even though God didn't ask our permission before he created our wills, he nonetheless created our wills free. If he can create a free will without its permission, he can also make it even freer without its permission. The important point is that freer is what he makes it.

Unfortunately, Calvinists have often obscured all this by the way we talk about the work of the Spirit. We have been anxious to emphasize that when the Spirit works the new birth in our hearts, he does not discover a prior willingness on our part and build upon that as a starting point. Nor does he (as some have claimed) start working in us, and then either continue or withdraw based on whether we accept or resist his work. The Calvinist view is that a willingness to be worked on by the Spirit is always and immediately the fruit of the Spirit's work, so it's logically impossible, even in principle, to speak of that work as ever being resisted. Hence, the "five points of Calvinism" describe the work of the Spirit as "irresistible," because no resistance can in fact take place. Hence, Calvinistic apologists often point out that the Greek word used to describe the work of the Spirit in John 6:44 is elsewhere used to refer to actions like physically pulling or dragging. These and similar approaches, though appropriate in limited doses, can give occasion for the misunderstanding that Calvinists picture the human will struggling vainly against the Spirit and then being violently overcome, routed, captured, and enslaved. But that is not what Calvinism pictures at all.

For the record, Jonathan Edwards did *not* compare the work of the Spirit to rape. The phrase "a holy rape of the surprised will" was coined in a 1943 article by historian Perry Miller to describe what he (Miller) thought the doctrine of the work of the Spirit in some seventeenth-century New England Puritan writings amounted to.[4]

And yet . . . why would so many people, including many Calvinists, find it plausible that Edwards would say such a despicable thing—and mean it as praise!—if not because we Calvinists have done a poor job expressing what we really think about the new birth? I believed in this story myself until I started doing the research for this book, so I'm not claiming to be Mr. Knows-Everything-about-Theological-History. But the mere fact that so many people find this story believable speaks volumes about the state of Calvinistic theological discourse.

3. Calvinism does not say we are totally depraved.

The "five points of Calvinism," at least in their twentieth-century form, begin with the assertion that human beings, in their natural state, are "totally depraved." But just as the phrase "free will" meant something completely different in the sixteenth-century Reformation debate than it does today, the phrase "totally depraved" in the five points doesn't mean what it would mean if somebody used that phrase in everyday conversation. In that sense, which is the sense that matters, Calvinism strongly denies "total depravity."

The five points use the phrase "total depravity" in a misleading, technical, counter-intuitive way. And unlike the case of "free will," in this case there is no good excuse for the confusion. Embarrassingly, the five points begin with this misleading phrase so that the first point will begin with the letter *T* in order to form the acrostic TULIP. Never has so much theological confusion been so widely sown for so trivial a reason!

When people hear the assertion that apart from the regeneration of the Holy Spirit we are "totally depraved," they naturally take that to mean there is nothing in us that is good in any respect. Besides being false to all experience, such a view is easy to disprove from Scripture. The Bible frequently notes the presence of qualities in unbelievers that are good in some way. Jesus calls the scribes and Pharisees hypocrites and declares that they lack justice and mercy and faithfulness, "the weightier matters of the law"—and in the same breath praises them for tithing scrupulously (Matt. 23:23). More generally, Paul declares that "Gentiles, who do not have the law, by nature do what the law requires" (Rom. 2:14). Perhaps most profoundly, we are admonished not to murder anyone because all people are made in the image of God (Gen. 9:6).

Moreover, if there were really nothing good in us, then we couldn't know right from wrong—since knowledge of righteousness would be something good. If that were the case, we wouldn't be culpable for sinning; it couldn't be our fault that we sin if we didn't know right from wrong. This seems to be exactly Paul's point in Romans 2, where after observing that the Gentiles "by nature do what the law requires," he goes on to comment that "they show that the work of the law is written on their hearts, while their conscience also bears witness" (Rom. 2:15).

But in fact, Calvinism doesn't say there's nothing in us that is good in any respect. This is clear even from the very first sentence of the Westminster Confession, which asserts (among other things) that fallen people are "unexcusable" because they have "the light of nature" to show them "the goodness, wisdom, and power of God." As we will see in more detail below, in its chapter "Of Good Works" the Confession also acknowledges that fallen people not only know right from wrong, but are able to serve their neighbors and do many other things God requires.

Calvin said the same:

> In every age there have been persons who, guided by nature, have striven toward virtue throughout life. I have nothing to say against them even if many lapses can be noted in their moral conduct. For they have by the very zeal of their honesty given proof that there was some purity in their nature. . . . These examples, accordingly, seem to warn us against adjudging man's nature wholly corrupted, because some men have by its prompting not only excelled in remarkable deeds, but conducted themselves most honorably throughout life. But here it ought to occur to us that amid this corruption of nature there is some place for God's grace; not such grace as to cleanse it, but to restrain it inwardly.[5]

Calvinism doesn't say fallen people are never good in any respect. It says fallen people are never completely and totally good—good in *every* respect. In our natural state, without regeneration from the Holy Spirit, we can never be the kind of good that God had in mind when he surveyed what he created and called each thing "good" (Genesis 1) or that Jesus had in mind when he said "Why do you call me good? No one is good except God alone" (Mark 10:18).

The matter becomes clearer when the Confession comes to the subject of Adam and Eve's original sin:

> By this sin they fell from their original righteousness and commu-
> nion with God, and so became dead in sin, and wholly defiled in all
> the parts and faculties of soul and body. (WCF 6.2)

"Dead in sin and wholly defiled in all parts" is a much clearer statement of what Calvinism teaches about the natural sinfulness of humanity.

The word "wholly" in "wholly defiled" may seem similar at first to the word "totally" in "totally depraved." And in fact, that's where the phrase "totally depraved" comes from. It was an attempt to rephrase "wholly defiled" so that it would begin with the letter *T* and thus fit the TULIP acronym.

But there's a critical difference. "Wholly" implies "all over, throughout, pervasively, everywhere." But "totally" implies "as much as possible, completely, ultimately, utterly." The phrase "in all parts" clinches the difference. The point is that all our "parts" are defiled, not that we are as defiled as we can be.

There is as much difference between being "wholly defiled" and being "totally depraved" as there is between being dirty all over and being dirt. It's not that we have no good things in us; it's that the good things God put in us have all become spoiled: our hearts, our intellects, our emotions, our desires, our wills, our bodies, our souls, our spirits. Every part of us is defiled—corrupt and ruined. And it's important to notice that the very concepts "defiled," "spoiled," "corrupt," and "ruined" can be applied only to something that was originally good and still retains its original goodness at least in some respects. What makes a thing defiled, spoiled, corrupt, or ruined is not that its original goodness has been annihilated, but that it has been redirected to evil purposes.

An unregenerate person can keep a promise. He can even keep a promise for the right reason, for the sake of the promise rather than because keeping it will profit him in some way. In doing so, he does what God commands and serves his neighbor. Those are both good things. But he doesn't do it with a heart that loves God or with a mind that knows God's revealed word or with a will that seeks

God's glory, and that means his promise-keeping is not "good" in the full and ultimate sense the Bible intends when it refers to "good works."

Calvinism says that everything in our fallen nature is hostile to the perfect goodness of God—to "goodness" in the absolute sense. This is not because our nature contains nothing that is good in any respect, but because everything in us is spoiled by our sin. In other words, Calvinism is saying that we are born as slaves to Satan—so we're right back to the "free will" issue again! We are born with every part of ourselves participating in, and hence defiled by, a state of freely chosen rebellion against God. (See the appendix, question 6.)

4. Calvinism does not deny that God loves the lost.

In each of the three cases above, people believe Calvinism says *x* when in fact Calvinism strenuously denies *x*. The question of whether God loves the lost, however, is different. Calvinism, in itself, implies no position one way or the other on this issue. Calvin himself didn't address it because the question hadn't been raised yet during his life. It was later generations of Calvinists, contemplating the Calvinistic doctrine, who started asking whether God loves those whom he has not chosen to save.

There are Calvinists who have all sorts of different opinions about this. Ask a hundred Calvinists whether God loves the lost and you will get a hundred different answers. Many of those answers will begin with yes; many will begin with no; many will begin with "we can't know the answer because he hasn't told us"; and many will begin with "I honestly have no idea what to think." But it's likely that no two answers will be exactly the same.

The issue was debated during the writing of the Westminster Confession. Ultimately, its authors chose not to have the Confession take any position on this issue. But they chose language that at least inclines toward the view that God loves the lost.[6] And some other historic Calvinist confessions, such as the Canons of Dort, explicitly endorse the view that God loves the lost, while no Calvinist confessions have ever explicitly endorsed the opposite view. This is more than enough to establish that Calvinism, simply as such, doesn't deny that God loves the lost, even if some Calvinists do.

Since this is a question Calvinists disagree about, it's especially important that I not open up a discussion of the technical issues here. What I want to make clear is that you can be a good Calvinist while believing very strongly that God loves the lost, or that he doesn't, or that we can't know, or while not knowing what to think, or while not thinking about the issue at all.

There is one more critical point that must be mentioned. One thing Calvinists all agree on is that God does not actively intervene in the wills of the lost in order to *make* them sin so that he can condemn them. The Westminster Confession insists that while God is active in choosing the saved for salvation, removing their judgment, and creating holiness in them, he is strictly passive in passing over the lost, permitting them to remain sinful and under judgment.[7] On the suggestion that God actively intervenes to cause lost people to reject him, R. C. Sproul—perhaps the most widely read Calvinist theologian of the twentieth century—justly comments:

> Such an idea was repugnant to Calvin and is equally repugnant to all orthodox Calvinists. The notion is sometimes called "hyper-Calvinism." But even that is an insult. This view has nothing to do with Calvinism. Rather than hyper-Calvinism, it is anti-Calvinism.[8]

5. Calvinism is not primarily concerned with the sovereignty of God or predestination.

If the last point was somewhat tricky to address, this one is even trickier. There is no absolute, unanswerable proof for what is or is not the "primary concern" of a theological tradition. It's a matter of judgment. Yet I think this issue is pretty clear cut if you make a serious study of Calvinism, so it's worth mentioning here. And the widely held idea that Calvinism is all about sovereignty and predestination is one of the most subtly destructive misperceptions of them all.

To be sure, Calvinism strongly affirms a particular view—a particularly "high" view, as such terms are used—of the sovereignty of God and predestination. But that view was not the unique and distinguishing theological contribution of Calvinism; nor was it the issue that Calvin or his followers (from that day to the present) thought was most important. Calvinism insists upon this particular view of sovereignty and predestination only as a necessary precaution against errors that would undermine other doctrines, and those other doctrines are Calvinism's real primary focus.

The "high" view of sovereignty and predestination was already fully worked out by Augustine in the early fifth century. All the important issues on this topic were aired during the debate between Christianity and the legalizing heresy of Pelagianism—and the endless bewildering variety of related movements, known as the "semi-Pelagian" heresies, that came after it. Pelagius argued that salvation is earned by good works; Augustine responded by showing that salvation is entirely a free gift of God's grace. The key dispute was over whose decision—God's or the believer's—effectively brought about salvation.

Not everyone in the church fully agreed with Augustine's position; in fact, by the early sixth century the church was already settling into a comfortable compromise that B. B. Warfield aptly dubbed "semi-semi-Pelagianism."[9] The important point, however, is that the "high" or thoroughly anti-Pelagian doctrine of sovereignty and predestination was fully formulated and systematically presented to the church not by Calvin but by Augustine eleven centuries before him.

Later generations of Augustinians would develop and debate different applications of that doctrine to other areas of theology. The most notable of these was Martin Luther, who worked out the connections between the Augustinian doctrine of sovereignty and predestination and the doctrine that our right standing with God comes by grace alone through faith alone in Christ alone. But on the doctrine of sovereignty and predestination simply in itself, subsequent theologians have added almost nothing to Augustine. On this topic, if we look past the superficial differences in tone and emphasis, there's not a dime's worth of difference between Augustine, Luther, and Calvin.

That's why, when sovereignty and predestination are the only issues on the table, it is common to hear this doctrine described as the "Augustinian" doctrine rather than the "Calvinist" doctrine. If Calvinism were primarily about this doctrine, it wouldn't be called Calvinism at all; it would just be Augustinianism. Calvin himself would be remembered only as an expositor of Augustine rather than as the father of a theological tradition in his own right. Or, more likely, he wouldn't be remembered as a theologian at all, since the great expositor of the Augustinian doctrine was really Luther, not Calvin.

What distinguishes Calvin as a theologian, and Calvinism as a theological tradition, is its uniquely "high" doctrine of the work of the Holy Spirit. In all the areas of theology where Calvin made his most distinguishing contributions, such as his doctrine of Scripture or his doctrine of the church and the sacraments, we see the exaltation of the work of the Spirit driving his analysis. Even if we look only at his understanding of salvation itself, what makes Calvinism uniquely Calvinistic is not primarily its doctrine of the work of the Father in election, but its doctrine of the work of the Spirit in regeneration.[10] And this predominance of the Spirit in Calvin's thought is mirrored throughout the Westminster Confession and other Calvinistic confessions and documents.

Of course, in Calvinism the Spirit does not rise to a level above the Father or the Son! Like all Western theological traditions, Calvinism holds that the Spirit proceeds from the Father and the Son, while neither the Father nor the Son proceeds from the Spirit.[11]

But while the Spirit does not get a place above the Father or the Son, he does get a much higher place in Calvinism than he got in the earlier Roman and Lutheran traditions, where his work got short shrift. And subsequent theological traditions have differentiated themselves from Calvinism primarily by their lower estimate of the importance of the Spirit's work (although they do still elevate the Spirit to a higher level of importance than either Rome or the Lutherans).

With its elevation of the Spirit's work alongside the work of the Father and Son, Calvinism fully brought out the consequences of the Trinity for Christian theology. In Calvinism, a distinctively high view of the work of the Father (Augustinian predestination) is integrated with a distinctively high view of the work of the Son (personal substitution) and a distinctively high view of the work of the Spirit (supernatural regeneration) to form an integrated Trinitarian whole. The Augustinian view is that all phenomena are from God (through predestination) and to God (because they all work together under God's sovereign control to manifest his glory). Calvinism takes this a step further. For the Calvinist, the whole Christian life, individually and collectively—salvation, worship, discipleship, and mission—is not only *from* God and *to* God but also *through* God in the overwhelming, all-encompassing, miraculous power of the Spirit. And the fully Trinitarian character of Calvinism preserves the stability of the whole; its high view of the work of each divine person upholds and protects its high view of the work of each of the others. This gives Calvinist theology coherence and stability.

It is this integrated theological whole, encompassing all phenomena through a fully Trinitarian account of God's work in all things, that is the real heart of Calvinism. As Warfield put it, "God fills the whole horizon of the Calvinist's feeling and thought."[12] He does so because the Calvinist sees all of God (all three persons) glorifying himself in all phenomena.

By contrast, the aforementioned chapter 3 of the Westminster Confession, asserting the Augustinian doctrine of sovereignty and predestination, abruptly issues this stern warning:

> The doctrine of this high mystery of predestination is to be handled with special prudence and care, that men, attending the will of God revealed in his Word, and yielding obedience thereunto, may, from the certainty of their effectual vocation, be assured of their eternal election. So shall this doctrine afford matter of praise, reverence, and admiration of God; and of humility, diligence, and abundant consolation to all that sincerely obey the gospel. (WCF 3.8)

This is not the kind of thing one normally finds in a confessional document. The purpose of a confession is to confess things, not to issue warnings about how dangerous it is to confess them for the wrong reason. I'm not aware of any other confessional document that contains a warning like this. And no other doctrine in the Westminster Confession is accompanied by such a warning.

Amazingly, the authors of the Confession refuse to take a back seat to anyone in asserting that it's spiritually dangerous to make predestination your central theological concern. This doctrine is to be confessed, they admonish us, for the limited purpose of helping believers form a godly assurance of their salvation through self-emptying humility before God's majesty. Under those conditions, and only those, the doctrine of predestination encourages reverence and meekness. Those who make predestination the core of their theology, we are left to infer, are setting themselves up for the opposite result—self-righteous pride. No Roman, Lutheran, or Arminian ever repudiated an obsession with predestination more firmly than the authors of the Westminster Confession.

Beyond the Superficial

Admittedly, everything I've said here is very superficial. But that's because I'm responding to very superficial errors. These deep theological topics invite us to enter into the contemplation of God with a rich depth of seriousness and vulnerability. Simple and superficial answers can never be sufficient for us to really encounter God in these things. But we can't get to the level of depth and nuance until we first clear away the more gross and simplistic misunderstandings.

In other words: if you think that everything I've said here is oversimplified to the point of being pat, ham-handed, and glib—I agree! My only point has been that the simple preconceptions almost everyone brings to these questions are insufficient. With that out the way, we can get to the really interesting stuff.

1

God Loves You Personally

When Jesus died and rose again, he saved you.

Let me ask you a question. Do you love humanity? Now let me ask you another question. Do you demonstrate love to every person you meet?

Almost everybody "loves humanity." It's easy to "love humanity." In fact, it's much easier than loving any particular individual person—even a person you're naturally inclined toward. Myself, I find it much easier to "love humanity" than to love my best friends, my spiritual family in the church, my daughter, or even my wife. After all, these people frequently annoy me, defy me, and make demands on my time and energy; "humanity" never does any of that. And these are the people I actually want to love! As for loving my enemies—well, give me "humanity" any day of the week.

Of course, the reason it's so easy to "love humanity" is that we never actually have to deal with "humanity" in real life. We only have to deal with individual people. And you know what *they're* like.

This is just another way of saying that "loving humanity" is easy because *it doesn't require you to love*. A pastor of mine once said that love is not an emotion; love is a way of behaving. And it's a pretty difficult, strenuous form of behavior under most circumstances! The emotional experience—the feeling—that we call love is supposed to come to us as the byproduct of loving behavior. It's partly a support that helps us do the behavior and partly a reward for doing the behavior. To make the emotion the main thing you care about, and put the behavior second—or worse, to want the emotion without the behavior at all—is selfish and deeply wicked. Yet that's what we all tend to do.

When we separate the emotion of love from loving behavior in our real relationships, things go off the rails pretty quickly. We get conflicts, we get coldness, we get resentment, we get betrayal. Above all, we discover that the emotional experience of love, which we wanted so badly, has itself disappeared or radically diminished.

That's what's so great about "loving humanity." Because it's not a real relationship, there's nothing to go off the rails. You can sit there wallowing in the emotion, just like a pig in filth, without ever lifting a finger for anybody, and you never pay a price.

That's why, when I write ironically about "loving humanity," I don't just put the word "humanity" in sarcastic scare quotes. I put the word "loving" in sarcastic scare quotes, too. When you "love humanity," not only do you not really deal with humanity, but you don't really love. Real love is personal. Real love is doing concrete things for concrete individuals.

The Personal Intimacy of God's Love

If that's the way it is for us, how much more so for God? God's love is always real love, so God's love is always personal. To begin with, because God is perfect, he doesn't try to cheat the system the way we do. When he feels the emotion of love, it's always because he's doing the behavior. And he always knows that the behavior is what really counts.

But although God's love is personal, it's not as personal as ours. It's much *more* personal than ours!

Think about it: how well do you really know other people? You can't read minds. You can't read hearts. You can't read spirits. The vast majority of what's going on inside other people—even the people you're closest to—is a complete mystery to you. In fact, you don't know about or understand half of the mental, emotional, and spiritual things going on inside yourself! So consider how little you really know about other people.

48

It's not that way for God. He knows it all. The people he loves are completely transparent to him. And they are transparent not just at one point but across time. Before God even made you, he already knew every single thing you were ever going to do, say, think, feel, wish, or imagine over the whole course of your life.

And this knowledge is not abstract, like something written down on a piece of paper that God reads, or even something God just knows intellectually, "in his head." God is not remote from us. He's fully present in every particle of creation. The entirety of the infinite God is inside you right now. He knows you with a closeness so intimate we can't even begin to imagine it. A mother breastfeeding her newborn child or a married couple joined in the conjugal act don't have anything even remotely like the closeness to one another that God has with you right at this moment.

And this intimacy is not just at this moment but at every moment. It can never be any other way. God cannot stop being God, so he can't stop being all-knowing and all-present. God's love is always personal. He doesn't have any other kind of love to give, because any other kind of love would not be the love of a God who was God.

That God knows us so completely and intimately is, of course, what makes it so amazing that he loves us so much—given how horrible the things going on in us are. In our saving relationship with Jesus, do we love Jesus personally? How much more must Jesus love us personally?

Jesus has done—and is still doing—so much for us that it is difficult to really believe he did all of it for each one of us personally, because he loves each of us personally. But it's true. And if we want to understand Jesus's work in saving us, then we need to get this clear and keep it clear. When Jesus created the universe; when Jesus guarded, guided, and governed his chosen people for thousands of years; when Jesus "emptied himself" and became a man; when Jesus bore years and years of servitude; when Jesus suffered under Pontius Pilate; when Jesus was crucified, dead, and buried;

when Jesus descended into hell on the cross; when Jesus rose again from the dead and ascended into heaven; when Jesus sits at the right hand of God the Father almighty, making intercession for us and advocating our cause—all this he did for you, personally. All along, as he did each and every act, he knew you completely and intimately. Each and every thing he did, he did to save you, personally.

He was doing it for you so personally that it would not have been any more personal if he had actually announced your name at each step. "Moses, I am sending you to tell Pharaoh to let my people go for the sake of Stephen Ford, born in Fairfax, Virginia, on October 6, 1973, so that he will become my adopted brother, be cleansed of his sin, and come into the blessedness of my kingdom forever and ever."

The Horrible Implication

Why do we find this so difficult to keep in our heads? Why do we have such a tendency to depersonalize the love of God?

No doubt it's partly just our inability to fully understand anything about the infinite God. We struggle to grasp even the most limited aspects of God's being as it really is. And when we have struggled and struggled, we understand so little that we're still overwhelmed by the mystery. Limited minds like ours just can't keep everything we know about God always at the center of our attention. And since we're not just limited but lazy and self-centered, it's no wonder if we habitually slide back into more limited conceptions of God. They're so much easier, so much more comfortable.

But I think there's another reason we tend to shrink from seeing God's love as personal. It's because God doesn't save every person.

If we picture Jesus doing all of his work for us personally, and we also know that not every person is saved by Jesus's work, the natural and obvious conclusion is that Jesus does not do his saving work for all people. We may say that Jesus loves those he doesn't save, even loves them personally, in some other way. But we could not say that Jesus's saving love—the love that does the work of salvation—was exercised on behalf of the lost.

In fact, since Jesus knows the lost every bit as completely and as intimately as he knows his own people, the exclusion of the lost from Jesus's saving work would also have to be a personal exclusion. It would have to be as though Jesus said, at every step of his work, "Moses, I am *not* sending you to tell Pharaoh to let my people go on behalf of Jason Rutledge, born in Omaha, Nebraska, on March 17, 1965. I am not doing anything to make him my brother, cleanse him, or bring him into my kingdom. He is lost forever, because I have not chosen him."

We recoil in horror—I do as much as you—from this thought. At first blush, everything in us seems to rise up in unison against any such suggestion. That's why, for thousands of years, Christian theologians have struggled to find some way to articulate how Jesus could do saving work on behalf of all people, and yet the lost remain lost.

Depersonalizing God's Love

All the attempts to solve this problem begin by depersonalizing God's saving love. They can't help but do so; there is simply no getting around it. Because God is all-powerful, whatever he tries to do must succeed. Any "solution" to a theological problem that pictures God attempting to do something and failing must go right out the window. Whatever work God sets his hand to must be effective. But if God wants to save all individuals personally, and God always accomplishes what he wants, then all individuals must be saved—which we know isn't true.

So the only way to solve this problem is to say that God's saving love is not directed at individuals personally. If we want to say God does not exclude specific individuals personally, then we must also say he does not save specific individuals personally. If the saving is personal, the excluding must also be personal. Therefore if we want God's saving work to be universal, it cannot be personal.

And, in fact, this is precisely what all the proposed solutions to the problem do say, in one way or another.

This is the first and most fundamental dividing line between Calvinism and all other theological traditions. Everything else that divides Calvinism from non-Calvinism is merely a consequence of this first and fundamental division. The Calvinist, seeing that the only way to "solve" this theological problem is to depersonalize the love of God, pulls back and refuses to do so. All others press on, accepting the depersonalization of God's saving love. If it means they can avoid accepting the horrible thought that God chooses to exclude specific people from salvation, then depersonalizing God's love is a price they're willing to pay.

Every tradition besides Calvinism claims that God's saving love is aimed not at particular individuals but at humanity in the mass. God may well love individuals as individuals, personally. But that aspect of his love is not what saves people. Jesus did not die on the cross and rise again from the dead because he loved you personally—loving you, the individual whom he knows completely and intimately. He did it because he loves people in general, in the abstract.

In short, Jesus died on the cross and rose from the dead because he "loves humanity."

It is important to clearly grasp the difference between saying God loves all people—loves each of them personally, as individuals—and saying God "loves humanity" in the abstract. It is one thing to say God loves you personally, and also loves me personally, and also loves this person, and that person . . . and so on until we have included every individual in the whole human race from Adam to the last person born at the end of history. It is a very different thing to say God "loves" the theoretical concept of "humanity"—that he loves the abstraction, the mass as mass, impersonally.

At the risk of trying your patience, I must insist on pressing this point. Everything else in this book hangs on it. All theological traditions besides Calvinism claim the saving "love" for "humanity" that led Jesus up to the cross and down to the grave, and then back up out of it, is a love that does not embrace any specific individuals at all. If it did, that would put us right back where we started with our problem. If the love that led Jesus to the cross is a love for any individual people, then either it is a love for all individual people or only for some. We don't want it to be only for some, because that thought is horrible. But if it's for all people then either they're all saved (which we know is not true) or God's work fails in its purpose (which we also know is not true). So God's saving love is either a personal love that embraces some and not others, or it is not a personal love at all; it embraces no individuals. It is entirely abstract.

Offering Salvation Systems
Depersonalizing God's love has far-reaching consequences. If God's saving love is impersonal, it follows that Jesus's saving work—even his death on the cross and his resurrection—do not actually save any individual person. When Jesus died and rose again, he did not accomplish anyone's salvation. If he had, this would imply his saving work had personally applied to that individual.

We can't have it both ways. Jesus's death and resurrection do not actually save you unless you, personally, are the object of their effectiveness. And if Jesus died and rose again not for you personally, but for "humanity," then his death and resurrection by themselves have no personal effectiveness for you. How could they, when they were not done for you?

Instead, the most we can possibly say on this view is that Jesus's saving work makes salvation available. And that is what all theological traditions besides Calvinism do say. In their various ways, they portray the saving work of Jesus as creating a system of salvation. All it does is create the system. Jesus does his work to make salvation available. Individuals are not actually saved until they avail themselves of the salvation system through some other process.

In the Roman tradition, the salvation system Jesus created is the church—not the church in the sense of all believers, but the church as a concrete institution, what has traditionally been called the "visible church." You get plugged into the salvation system through the ordinances of the visible church, especially through the sacraments. You first receive salvation in the sacrament of baptism, which is the basis of your justification; you build up your holiness through both faith and good works, especially by participating in the sacrament of the Mass; and you remove the guilt of your sins by confessing them and performing compensatory works in the sacrament of penance.

In the Lutheran tradition, the salvation system Jesus created is the "means of grace," especially the gospel but also including the sacraments of baptism and the Lord's Supper. You get plugged into the salvation system by using the means of grace—most importantly by believing the gospel, but also by using the other means. The relationship between the gospel and the other means of grace has been a subject of much debate in Lutheran circles, but they all agree that the only way to be saved is through the means of grace.

In the various Arminian traditions, the salvation system Jesus created is simply the gospel. You get plugged into the salvation system by believing. Your salvation is accomplished when you are confronted with the gospel and make your choice to believe—or else not. Different Arminian systems have different theologies of this moment of decision; for example, they integrate it in different ways with the work of the Holy Spirit. But for all of them, it is the moment of decision that saves you.

When we discuss the differences between theological traditions, these are the differences we tend to focus on. What is the salvation system we need to use? Is it the sacraments? Belief? The "means of grace"? Yet the most important issue is usually overlooked. Are you saved by a salvation system or by Jesus himself? That is the difference between Calvinism and all other systems.

Personal Substitution
I call this the most important issue because it creates a deep and radical difference in how we view the work of Jesus. It is the differ-

ence between the man who manufactures life vests and the man who pulls drowning people out of the water, between the man who makes a scalpel and the man who uses it to cut out a cancerous tumor and save a patient's life.

Creating a system to do something is a fundamentally different thing from actually doing it. Thus, saying that Jesus creates a salvation system rather than saving us gives us a fundamentally different perspective on the cross and the empty tomb.

The people who make life vests and surgical scalpels are of course doing important and worthy work. But we don't give them nearly the honor we give to the people who actually save lives— and rightly so. Thus, if we change our conception of Jesus from the person who saves us to the person who creates the salvation system, our esteem for his work must change as well.

The issues at stake here could not be more vital. Historically, Christianity has taught that Jesus saves you by acting as your substitute. He stood in your place and did for you what you could not do; he bore the guilt, and therefore the divine wrath, that you had stored up for yourself. By doing so, he purchased for you a place in God's kingdom.

Substitution is essential to the scriptural witness on Jesus's work. The prophets insist on it: "He was wounded for our transgressions; he was crushed for our iniquities; upon him was the chastisement that brought us peace, and with his stripes we are healed" (Isa. 53:5). Paul insists on it: "For our sake he made him to be sin who knew no sin, so that in him we might become the righteousness of God" (2 Cor. 5:21). Peter insists on it: "He himself bore our sins in his body on the tree, that we might die to sin and live to righteousness. By his wounds you have been healed" (1 Pet. 2:24).

Since the substitutionary view of Jesus's work is so important to the biblical account of salvation, all theological traditions seek to integrate the substitutionary view with the rest of their theology. Obviously this integration is especially important to the topic of how Jesus's work relates to the individual believer.

It is the very essence of substitution that it is personal. It would be nonsense to talk about Jesus saving you by becoming the substitute of an abstract concept. If you are to be saved by Jesus's death and resurrection, he must do these things as *your* substitute; he must take *your* place. A substitutionary act must be aimed at persons, or it is not substitutionary at all.

Here, the claim—made by all traditions except Calvinism—that Jesus did his saving work impersonally comes squarely into conflict with any meaningful concept of substitutionary atonement. To avoid the Calvinistic conclusion, all other traditions have to say that Jesus's saving work is not aimed at any particular people. It cannot be aimed at "all humanity" in the sense of being aimed at each individual person in the whole human race. It must be aimed at "all humanity" as an abstract concept, without reaching any individual people at all. And this means it cannot be, in itself, an act of substitution. If Jesus's work only makes salvation available, then it cannot be substitutionary in any meaningful sense.

The most common way of getting around this difficulty is to say that Jesus's death and resurrection are "hypothetically" or "conditionally" substitutionary. Jesus dies and rises again in the place of all humanity on the hypothesis, or on the condition, that they will get plugged into the salvation system—by receiving the sacraments, or the means of grace, or the gospel. Thus, Jesus can personally substitute for every person; not actually, but hypothetically or conditionally.

This view creates several problems. Perhaps the most important is that it totally removes the act of substitution from Jesus's work. A substitution occurs, but Jesus does not accomplish it. Jesus dies on the cross and rises from the dead, not for you, but for some hypothetical or conditional version of you. Then, apart from Jesus's work, through the salvation system that Jesus creates, you become the hypothetical or conditional version of yourself for whom Jesus died.

That process, not Jesus's work, accomplishes the act of substitution. When you receive baptism, or when you believe the gospel, or when you plug into the salvation system in some other way, that is the moment Jesus's righteousness is substituted for your sins.

In this view, the cross and the empty tomb provide neither the basis nor the mechanism of the substitution. The mechanism of the substitution is the salvation system. The basis of the substitution is whatever it was—baptism, belief, etc.—that plugged you into the system.

The staggering conclusion is that, in this view, Jesus's work does not remove your sins. If it did, it would actually save you. And then we'd be right back on the merry-go-round—if Jesus died for all people, and his work removed the sins of those for whom he died, everyone would be saved. All traditions besides Calvinism have gotten off the merry-go-round only by denying—in effect, if not in so many words—that Jesus's work removes your sins.

No Hypotheticals

Yet even this argument is giving these theories too much credit. Just to state the case that these views remove substitution from Jesus's work, we have had to make an assumption in their favor. We have had to accept the idea that a "hypothetical" or "conditional" version of you is possible for God. In fact, it is not. God is all knowing. Nothing is hypothetical or conditional for him. When Jesus climbs up on the cross, he knows full well who will be saved and who won't. How can we say that he sacrifices himself on the assumption of a hypothesis he knows to be false, or on a condition he knows is not met?

But we are not done yet. Now we must ask: If the cross is not for substitution, why was it necessary at all? If God wanted to remove people's sins by using a system composed of sacraments, belief, or some combination thereof, why did he need to send his Son to the cross to create that system?

If there is to be any meaningful answer to this question, some other obstacle to salvation besides our sins and the need for substitution must be found. The most plausible response you could make, without surreptitiously smuggling in a personal substitution, is that it would have been inconsistent with God's character to save us without first manifesting his wrath against the sins of humanity. Jesus's work is not, in itself, substitutionary; he does not bear the actual wrath stored up for particular people, because that would drag us back to the merry-go-round. Rather, the general nature of God's governance of the universe required a display of wrath.

Thus, Calvinist theologians have often argued that the highest and most important role that any system other than Calvinism can consistently give to the cross is what has traditionally been called the "governmental" theory of atonement. It is called that because it locates the need for the atonement not in the bearing of any individual's personal sins, but in God's desire to maintain good government in the universe generally. And if my non-Calvinist brothers and sisters will forgive me, I cannot refrain from observing that the "governmental" view of Jesus's work does fit perfectly with the depersonalized view of God's love. Jesus did an impersonal work on behalf of an abstraction, for the sake of a general principle.

Now, it is important to note that the non-Calvinist theological traditions do not actually profess the governmental view. They deny it strenuously. And I don't doubt their sincerity for a moment. I fully believe that they reject it as firmly as I do.

However, I think that when they reject it, they are contradicting themselves. Their initial depersonalization of God's love, if they remained faithful to it and worked it out to its necessary conclusions, would lead them directly to the governmental view. I'm grateful that they contradict themselves in order to affirm substitutionary atonement. But contradicting themselves is, in fact, what they are doing.

Salvation at the Cross and the Tomb

Over against all this, Calvinism—alone among theological traditions—upholds the personal nature of God's saving love and safeguards the effectiveness of Jesus's saving work. Jesus died and rose again for you, personally; and when he did, he actually saved you, personally.

Of course, while salvation is accomplished at the cross and the empty tomb, it doesn't start there and it doesn't remain there. Salvation involves believing the gospel. "I told you that you would die in your sins, for unless you believe that I am he you will die in your sins" (John 8:24). Salvation involves receiving the Holy Spirit. "Can anyone withhold water for baptizing these people, who have received the Holy Spirit just as we have?" (Acts 10:47). Salvation involves being known and chosen by God the Father before the foundation of the world. "Blessed be the God and Father of our Lord Jesus Christ, who has blessed us in Christ with every spiritual blessing in the heavenly places, even as he chose us in him before the foundation of the world, that we should be holy and blameless before him" (Eph. 1:3–4). Salvation involves dying to sin and turning to a new and holy life characterized by discipleship, obedience, and diligent service to others. "If we say we have fellowship with him while we walk in darkness, we lie and do not practice the truth" (1 John 1:6). And salvation involves the final judgment, glorification, and entrance into the new earth that will only come at the end of history. "Do you not know that in a race all the runners run, but only one receives the prize? So run that you may obtain it" (1 Cor. 9:24). That's why Scripture sometimes refers to salvation in the past tense (e.g., Luke 7:50; Eph. 2:8; 2 Tim. 1:9; Titus 3:5), sometimes in the present tense (e.g., 1 Cor. 1:18; 2 Cor. 3:18; Phil. 2:12), and sometimes in the future tense (e.g., Rom. 5:9; 1 Cor. 5:5; 1 Thess. 5:8; 1 Pet. 1:5).

But while salvation involves all these things, none of them accomplishes our salvation. The actual *saving* happens at the cross and at the empty tomb. Everything that comes before is preparing for the accomplishment of salvation. Everything that comes afterward is working out the effects of its accomplishment.

Wherever we turn, the Scriptures never describe Jesus's work as making salvation available. They say Jesus actually saves us. "She will bear a son, and you shall call his name Jesus, for he will save his people from their sins" (Matt. 1:21). "Grace to you and peace from God our Father and the Lord Jesus Christ, who gave himself for our sins to deliver us from the present evil age" (Gal. 1:3–4). "For as by the one man's disobedience the many were made sinners, so by the one man's obedience the many will be made righteous" (Rom. 5:19). "In this is love, not that we have loved God but that he loved us and sent his Son to be the propitiation for our sins" (1 John 4:10).

Once we have said that we are actually saved in the cross and the empty tomb, we have given up any right to say that the effectiveness of Jesus's work is determined either by the sacraments or by our decision to believe the gospel. Once again, we can't have it both ways. Either Jesus saves us, or else he only makes salvation available, leaving it for us to avail ourselves of salvation.

The Calvinist will not say, "Jesus makes salvation available and then I avail myself of it," because he sees that this is really the same as saying that Jesus doesn't save us; indeed, it is just a hair's breadth away from saying that we save ourselves. For once we make the effectiveness of the cross and the tomb subject to some subsequent process, we have emptied them of substitution, and with substitution all the substance of our salvation. And once we deny that Jesus determines the effectiveness of his own work, we make its effectiveness subject to our actions, thus attributing the outcome of salvation to ourselves (in effect if not in so many words).

Few would disagree with the statement that a true Christian is a person who clings for salvation, not to the church; not to the sacraments; not to the Bible; not even to the proclamation of the gospel or the believer's belief in it; but to the cross and the empty tomb. Calvinism is just the systematic application of this truth in all doctrine, piety, and life. If you make this truth your theological touchstone and resolve to reject everything that comes into conflict with it, and carry out that resolution consistently, you will find yourself a Calvinist.

The Hinge of Salvation

Let me pause here to offer a clarification. I've already noted that there are many different steps involved in salvation, and clearly they take place at different times. God's choosing of me to be one of his people takes place before the beginning of the world; his transformation of my nature as part of the making of the new heavens and the new earth takes place at the end of history. Obviously no one is saying that Jesus accomplishes all these steps in the cross and the empty tomb.

To describe all these different steps, theologians use many different terms: election, justification, adoption, regeneration, sanctification, purification, glorification, etc. Theological discussions of Jesus's work often focus on breaking down the process of salvation into these different steps and then describing how all the different pieces fit together.

I have not done that here. I will do some of it in later chapters. We will need to distinguish, for example, between justification (which makes us righteous in the sight of God) and sanctification (which makes us conformed to the holiness of God). Those distinctions are important.

But here at the beginning I have felt the need to talk about salvation as a single thing. While Scripture does warrant the discussion of all these different aspects of salvation separately, it also clearly warrants the discussion of salvation as a single thing. That's what I think we need to start with.

What is the center of salvation? What is its focal point, its locus? What is the hinge on which salvation turns? What is the tipping point at which the scales move, the size at which we achieve critical mass, the speed at which we have reached terminal velocity? What is the bedrock of our salvation?

For the Calvinist, the center of salvation is Jesus's work on the cross and in the empty tomb. Everything else that is a part of my salvation is only a part of my salvation because Jesus died and rose again for me. It is Jesus's work that really decides the issue. For all other traditions, the means by which we get plugged into the salvation system are the center of salvation. Everything else that is a part of my salvation is only a part of my salvation because I made a decision for Christ, or used the sacraments, or in some other way got plugged into Jesus. My getting plugged in is what really decides the issue.

Struggling to Truly Worship

The different conceptions of Jesus's work offered by the different theological traditions produce fundamentally different religious lives. The direction and focus of our devotion are inevitably shaped by whether we locate the pivotal hinge of our salvation in Jesus's work or in our receiving of that work.

This difference is most obvious between Protestant and Roman religious lives. While its pastors and leaders often labor mightily to direct people's attention to Jesus and his work, the locus of most people's devotion in the Church of Rome is constantly flowing away from Jesus. The Roman doctrine that we receive salvation through the sacraments is the main cause of this. In the best cases, devotion wavers back and forth between Jesus and the church, Mary, the saints, the sacraments, etc. In the worst cases, the sacraments become magical spells of purification that allow us to indulge headlong in our sins while feeling that we are right before God because we chant the right incantations. Labor as they do to hold up Jesus—and God bless them for it—the bishops of Rome can never get clear of this problem because it is embedded in their theology.

Yet the same problem is widely evident even in evangelical and Protestant religion, including in many churches that profess to be Calvinist. The joy of having peace with God is in constant competition with anxiety and fear because people feel that their possession of that peace is dependent on their own devotion. They think they're saved by their decision to believe, so they become obsessed with reinforcing their own belief. By whipping up frenzies of mass emotion, or through more subtle methods of mental and emotional manipulation, they constantly seek to reassure themselves that they do, they really do, have the peace of God.

This is what the Bible calls "will worship"—translated in the English Standard Version as "self-made religion"—worship that is not the natural outpouring of love from a transformed and grateful heart, but whipped up by force of will for some extraneous reason (Col. 2:23). This particular kind of will worship is especially subtle. Instead of inventing new religious forms, it takes the religious forms God gave us and ruthlessly exploits them for its own purposes.

Everything is different when we keep the locus of salvation at the cross and the tomb. Such moments are all too rare for fallen and sinful creatures like us, regardless of our theology. But it is only in those moments when we worship not by force of will, but as a natural and spontaneous outpouring of reverence and gratitude at the mighty work Jesus has done, and continues to do, for us and within us. Rather than trying to whip ourselves into a given mental state by force, as though a mental state were what God really valued in us, true worship is simply contemplating what God has done and responding to that knowledge in the way we naturally respond to it, if we are really loving him.

All Christians want a religious life that reflects their trust in the cross and the empty tomb as the things that save them. But most of them don't have it most of the time. That's mainly because the only solid and stable basis for such a religious life is a theology that teaches you to trust that the cross and the empty tomb have already saved you.

How Does God Love?

The personal nature of God's saving love is no less a treasure than the actual effectiveness of Jesus's saving work. It is just as precious a treasure because it is, ultimately, the same treasure. Nothing is more fundamental to Christianity than God's love for us. All other religions are either religions of law, in which we earn God's favor by deserving it, or else religions of negation, in which we learn to abandon our desire for God's favor on grounds that God has no favor to give—because he is too all-encompassing to favor one part of himself over another, or because he is too transcendent to care, or because he doesn't exist. Only Christianity holds that God's love, not his law or his negation, is fundamental.

The promises of God's love pervade the Bible. Throughout the Old Testament, God's care for his people is constantly attributed to his "steadfast love"—a very specific term used to denote God's special love for his particular people. And in the New Testament, everything from Jesus's work on our behalf to our response of faith and living into the Christian life is referred back to God's love for us:

> Beloved, let us love one another, for love is from God, and whoever loves has been born of God and knows God. Anyone who does not love does not know God, because God is love. In this the love of God was made manifest among us, that God sent his only Son into the world, so that we might live through him. In this is love, not that we have loved God but that he loved us and sent his Son to be the propitiation for our sins. Beloved, if God so loved us, we also ought to love one another. No one has ever seen God; if we love one another, God abides in us and his love is perfected in us. (1 John 4:7–12)

Because salvation, faith, the Christian life, and all good things come from God's love, it makes all the difference in the world how we conceive of this love. When the Bible says God loves us, is that a personal love for you and me or an abstract love for people in general?

It's not hard to find Scripture's answer to this question. From the Old Testament to the New, God's saving love is personal. "The LORD set his heart in love on your fathers and chose their offspring after them, you above all peoples, as you are this day" (Deut. 10:15). The special term "steadfast love" in the Old Testament that refers particularly to God's saving love for his people is used in a way that indicates it is a personal love. For example: "Great salvation he brings to his king, and shows steadfast love to his anointed, to David and his offspring forever" (2 Sam. 22:51).

In the gospels, Jesus's saving love is personal: "Having loved his own who were in the world, he loved them to the end" (John 13:1). When Jesus is preparing his followers to carry on after his death, he first says his saving love for them is just like his Father's personal love for him: "As the Father has loved me, so have I loved you" (John 15:9). He commands them to love one another, not because he loves people in general, but because he loves them particularly: "This is my commandment, that you love one another as I have loved you" (John 15:12). He then immediately emphasizes the point that his saving love for them is personal: "Greater love has no one than this, that someone lay down his life for his friends" (John 15:13). He then prays, in the High Priestly Prayer, "that the world may know that you sent me and loved them even as you loved me" (John 17:23).

But the personal quality of God's saving love is most strongly emphasized in the apostolic Epistles. Consider Paul's opening remarks to the Ephesians:

> Blessed be the God and Father of our Lord Jesus Christ, who has blessed us in Christ with every spiritual blessing in the heavenly places, even as he chose us in him before the foundation of the world, that we should be holy and blameless before him. In love he predestined us for adoption as sons through Jesus Christ, according to the purpose of his will, to the praise of his glorious grace, with which he has blessed us in the Beloved. In him we have redemption through his blood, the forgiveness of our trespasses, according to the riches of his grace, which he lavished upon us, in all wisdom and insight making known to us the mystery of his will, according to his purpose, which he set forth in Christ as a plan for the fullness of time, to unite all things in him, things in heaven and things on earth. (Eph. 1:3–10)

For more about God's love and specifically the question of whether God's love extends in the same way to all, see the appendix, questions 8 and 9.

Only Some, or None at All
The Calvinist view does imply that Jesus endured long years of servitude, endless days of imprisonment and torture, hour after hour

of unspeakable agony on the cross, separation from the Father, and the full torment of hell itself, and finally death and resurrection, "only" for the salvation of some people rather than for all. To put it more formally, Jesus made atonement only for the sins of those who are actually saved. If Jesus makes atonement for your sins, you are in fact saved; therefore if you are not saved, he didn't make atonement for your sins.

When the saving work of Jesus is under discussion, this aspect of the Calvinistic view is usually what is said to set it apart from all other views. The Calvinist view of Jesus's work, people say, is that it is "limited" to only some people. That aspect of the Calvinist view certainly is one way in which Calvinism can be distinguished from other views. And Calvinists have been active in defending that view as against other views that expand the scope of the atonement to all people.

But the only reason Calvinists insist on limiting the scope of the atonement is in order to ward off anything that would imply a limitation on its power. A theology certainly can make the atonement universal, but only by making it feeble. Calvinists insist on an atonement that saves some but not others because they know that the only possible alternative is an atonement that saves no one at all.

In a word, Calvinism declines to "solve" the problem of how God's saving love can be personal and extended to everybody, yet nonetheless not all are saved. There is no solution to that problem. What we know about the love of God and the cross of Christ compels us to say that God's saving love cannot, in fact, be extended to everybody. If we try to have everything, we end by having nothing.

The search for a universal saving love that doesn't save universally is a theological snipe hunt. It's like trying to represent God's love in a diagram by drawing it as a square circle. Try as you might, you can't do it. And because you can't draw the diagram, you not only can't justify your contention that God wants to save everybody, you can't even justify your contention that God saves anybody.

None of this makes the idea of God passing over the lost and allowing them to remain in their sins any less horrible to us. Calvinist theology shows us that this horrible truth must be accepted. It does not make it any less horrible.

Naturally, we want to know why God would want to save some but not others. Before we look at that question, though, we'll need to know more than just the first and most fundamental point—that God's saving love is personal. We need to know what kind of personal love it is.

2

God Loves You Unconditionally

Nothing is more important to your
heavenly Father than saving you.

In the last chapter I mentioned the saying of an old pastor of mine, that love is not a feeling but a way of behaving. From this, it follows that the test of whether you love something isn't how you feel about it. It's how you behave toward it.

All through college and graduate school, I thought I loved the academic life. I thought I was made for it, that God had called me to it, and that no other life could possibly satisfy me. (Calvin thought the same thing before he got the call to lead the church in Geneva, so I guess I'm in good company.) But when I got out of grad school, I couldn't get an academic teaching job. As the spring wore on into the summer, it looked like the best thing I could hope for was a postdoctoral fellowship, which is kind of low-wage, no-benefits consolation prize for newly minted PhDs who can't find jobs. But there was not much professional shame in that—the academic job market is so rough that lots of people take these "post-docs" and then go back on the market the next year.

The trouble was, my wife was working a full-time job to support us both while I was in school, and her health was starting to fail. We found out later she had a chronic illness; at the time, we only knew that she was frequently in pain, and would often drag herself home from work and drop straight into bed, still in her clothes. Taking a job outside academia would hurt my chances of getting in later, but I couldn't let my wife's situation go on. I needed a full-time job that would let her quit working, and I needed it now.

I took a job doing research and writing for a think tank. It was a lot of fun, but it wasn't what I really loved—or so I thought. So I went back on the academic job market. Once again, I didn't get a job. This time, though, I was offered a highly sought-after post-doc position working under a nationally famous professor at one of the most prestigious colleges in the world.

It was likely to be my last chance to get into the academic career track. And what a chance! But it was still a post-doc; the pay was minimal and there were no health benefits. My wife would have to go back to full-time work. Her health had improved dramatically after she quit work, but I knew that if I took this post-doc she'd be right back where she had been.

So I turned it down. I'd like to be able to say it was an easy decision. Given my wife's health, it should have been an easy decision. But it wasn't. This was giving up my last chance at my only dream for what I was going to do with my professional life.

Since then I've come to realize that the Lord had other plans for my life. The career twists and turns he led me through weren't meaningless. They equipped me with a unique combination of skills, which prepared me perfectly for my current job—a job that I do love, probably better than I would have loved academia.

But do you know what else? My wife knows I love her.

The real test of whether you love something is whether you'll give other things up for its sake. And the test of how much you love it is how much you're willing to give up.

Spiritual Priorities

Real love is all about setting priorities. And the really challenging thing to grasp is that it's not just about prioritizing the things we do love above the things we don't love. It's about prioritizing some things we love above other things we love.

Our natural tendency is to think about love as a binary on/off switch. There are some people and things you love and others you don't. In reality, the issue that matters is whether you love one thing more than another.

We see this constantly in the Bible. Just to take one of countless examples, Jesus doesn't tell people to love the kingdom of God and not love anything else. He says, "Seek first the kingdom of God and his righteousness, and all these things will be added to you" (Matt. 6:33). The word that's translated "first" here is *protos*, which implies "first" in the sense of first in priority, not necessarily first in time. You don't seek the kingdom of God for the first hour of the day, then other things for the rest of the day. Rather, you get your priorities in order so that the kingdom of God has first place in your life. You can love other things too, but your love for them must be subordinate to, and therefore ordered by, your love for the kingdom.

Or consider what Paul says to men about marriage. On the one hand, he calls on husbands to love their wives—to love them powerfully and tremendously, with extraordinary self-sacrifice. "Husbands, love your wives, as Christ loved the church and gave himself up for her" (Eph. 5:25). Yet he also warns us that the great danger of marriage is that we'll love our wives more than God. "The unmarried man is anxious about the things of the Lord, how to please the Lord. But the married man is anxious about worldly things, how to please his wife, and his interests are divided" (1 Cor. 7:32–34).

The danger here is not that we'll love our wives. It's not even that we'll love our wives too much. The danger is that we'll love God too little. And the way we know we're loving God too little is that we're putting our wives before him. There's no upper limit to how much we're called to love our wives, but we're always called to love God more and put him first.

Or consider that disturbing moment where Jesus tells us that "if anyone comes to me and does not hate his own father and mother and wife and children and brothers and sisters, yes, and even his own life, he cannot be my disciple" (Luke 14:26). Obviously "hate" here cannot mean any kind of ill will—we are required to love our families, honor our elders, and care for our households. "If anyone does not provide for his relatives, and especially for members of his household, he has denied the faith and is worse than an unbeliever" (1 Tim. 5:8). Rather, in Luke 14:26 "hate" means to place second in priority, to refuse to give any ground at all to our families when our loyalties to them come into conflict with our duties to God.

As C. S. Lewis observes, this passage becomes clearer when we consider it in light of Malachi 1:2–3, where God says: "I have loved Jacob but Esau I have hated." Lewis remarks:

> How is the thing called God's "hatred" of Esau displayed in the actual story? Not at all as we might expect. . . . From all we are told, Esau's earthly life was, in every ordinary sense, a good deal more blessed than Jacob's. It is Jacob who has all the disappointments, humiliations, terrors, and bereavements. But he has something which Esau has not. He is a patriarch. He hands on the Hebraic tradition, transmits the vocation and the blessing, becomes an ancestor of Our Lord. The "loving" of Jacob seems to mean the acceptance of Jacob for a high (and painful) vocation; the "hating" of Esau, his rejection. He is "turned down," fails to "make the grade," is found useless for the purpose. So, in the last resort, we must turn down or disqualify our nearest and dearest when they come between us and our obedience to God. Heaven knows, it will seem sufficiently to them like hatred.[1]

The Ethics of Love

What I'm offering here is far from a new or unique insight. In our human relationships, we rely on this principle all the time. When our family and friends are willing to make sacrifices for us, we take that as strong evidence that their love for us is great. When they don't, we feel unloved.

Here's a particularly striking example. Today, the institution of lifetime marriage is scoffed at everywhere except in conservative religious subcultures. But have you noticed that when people first fall in love, they experience a very strong and seemingly spontaneous desire to bind themselves to each other—and, particularly, to do so by swearing an oath to forsake all others? Even in an environment where young people are raised not to anticipate lifetime marriage, they continue to feel this desire to negate or exclude the possibility of all other partners, not just for the moment but in perpetuity. They actually have to exert themselves to restrain this desire, reminding themselves to be "sensible" and "rational"— and, of course, "progressive" and "modern." If they followed their natural desires, they'd get married instead of living together. That's because the very essence of love is a willingness to sacrifice other things for the beloved. (Hence the funny song in *The Sound of Music* about a couple who can't fall in love because they're so perfect for each other; there are no obstacles for them to overcome to prove their love to each other.)

This is not a new insight for Christian ethical thought, either. Especially in the West, Christian ethics has long considered the proper ordering of our loves as central presuppositions for basic ethical concepts like duty and virtue. It's a mistake to think of ethics as fundamentally about rules. You could never formulate enough rules, or formulate them with enough clarity and specificity, to serve as useful moral guides to real life. This is what Jesus was getting at when he said that lustful thoughts do not just lead to adultery but are themselves a form of adultery (Matt. 5:28). The point of the rule against adultery is not simply to forbid the evil act but to show us how our loves ought to be ordered. The main offense is not the act itself; it's the disordered love that leads to the act. Focusing on rules instead of loves is like cleaning the cup on the outside but leaving it dirty on the inside (Matt. 23:25–26).

At heart, ethics is not about rules but about whether you are making God first priority, and then (as a consequence) getting all your other priorities straightened out. Just as love is not about what you do and don't love, but what you love more and what you love less, ethics is not about what you are and aren't supposed to love, but about what you're supposed to love more and what you're supposed to love less.

We Are God's Top Priority

And yet, although this insight is not particularly novel, we rarely think about God's love this way. When it comes to our own natural loves—or even our own supernatural loves, which we experience because of the Spirit's work in us—we have no problem seeing that the central test of love is how we set priorities. But when we turn from our own loves to God's love, we don't apply this perspective.

We all know that the test of my love for God is whether I'm willing to sacrifice other things I love for God's sake. But the test of God's love for me is exactly the same. This should be obvious to Christians above all. What did God give up for us? His Son. And what does it prove that God gave up his Son for us? That he loves us. "He who did not spare his own Son but gave him up for us all, how will he not also with him graciously give us all things?" (Rom. 8:32).

Like us, God loves more than one thing; and like us, he orders his loves. God sets priorities, too. And we know God loves us because he makes us top priority.

God loves us more than everything else in the whole natural world. "What is man that you are mindful of him, and the son of man that you care for him? Yet you have made him a little lower than the heavenly beings and crowned him with glory and honor. You have given him dominion over the works of your hands; you have put all things under his feet" (Ps. 8:4–6; see also Job 7:17–18).

God loves us more than his own rulership of the universe, considered in its merely moral and legal aspect. Jesus could have stayed on the throne of heaven forever, but for our sakes he emptied himself and even became a slave. "Though he was in the form of God, [he] did not count equality with God a thing to be grasped, but made himself nothing, taking the form of a servant, being born in the likeness of men" (Phil. 2:6–7). He even took upon himself the guilt and punishment of our sins—a more profound surrender of his own position of lordship than the human imagination could have even conceived.

Of course, even in temporarily giving up his lordship in its merely moral and legal aspects, he gained a far deeper and more glorious lordship. He got back the same moral and legal lordship he had given up, but now it's only supplemental to a new and even more amazing servant-kingship in which he rules a people who are not only his people because he made them, but because he redeemed them. However, the thing to get straight is that he achieved this greater glory not because he selfishly craved more glory—for he did not count glory as a thing to be grasped—but *for our sakes* (Phil. 2:6).

God even loves us more than life itself. That's what the cross is all about.

God Gives Things Up

Why do we so often think about the mere fact that God loves us, rather than thinking about how he loves us more than anything else—when that's a far more astonishing fact? Millions of people cherish John 3:16, but I sometimes wonder if they don't read it as "God so loved the world, that he *sent* his only Son, that whoever believes in him should not perish but have eternal life." Why is our piety so slow to grasp the astonishing implications of the assertion that God didn't just send, but *gave* his only Son for us? Why aren't we continually amazed that God would willingly give up everything else in the whole natural order for our sakes?

Perhaps it's because we don't like to think about God giving things up. Maybe we're afraid it would compromise God's sovereignty over the universe, his character as the all-powerful God, if we said that God had to give up something that he loved. Certainly in our own lives when we set priorities between different things that we love, it's usually because we aren't able to get everything we want. We have to give up some things we want in order to get other things we want. We must never picture God that way—God can do everything he wants.

But it's one thing to talk about what you want and another thing to talk about what you love. God always gets what he wants, but what he wants is determined by the priorities he sets among the different things that he loves. Jesus is not compelled to the cross; he goes to the cross willingly. "Put your sword into its sheath; shall I not drink the cup that the Father has given me?" (John 18:11). "Do you think that I cannot appeal to my Father, and he will at once send me more than twelve legions of angels? But how then should the Scriptures be fulfilled, that it must be so?" (Matt. 26:53–54). In that sense, the cross is what he wants. However, he wants the cross only because he loves us, and the will of his Father, more than he loves his own life. If you doubt that he loves his own life, go back and reread his prayers at Gethsemane! But he willingly subordinates his love for his own life to his love for us and his Father.

All Things Work Together

I think there may also be another reason we don't usually think about God's love in terms of setting priorities and giving things up. We may be afraid to think about whether there are limits to that. Are there things God isn't willing to give up for us? Perhaps we want to think about God's love in binary yes/no terms so that we can picture it as something total, something that has no competitors. Thinking about God setting priorities implies he may not always put us first.

And that would be very plausible. God says things like, "For my own sake, for my own sake, I do it, for how should my name be profaned? My glory I will not give to another" (Isa. 48:11). That sure sounds like God has some priorities that are higher than us.

But we shouldn't be worried. The same God also said, through Paul, that "we know that for those who love God all things work together for good, for those who are called according to his purpose" (Rom. 8:28). There are several things to notice about this famous passage. One is that it applies only to "those who love God" and "are called according to his purpose." This promise is for believers. As a pastor of mine once said, if you *don't* love God, all things will work together against you! We'll return to that subject in just a moment.

Another thing to notice is that it says all things work together, not to give us what we want, but "for good." God often doesn't give us what we want. But that is no reason to conclude God has weighed our good against some other priority and has decided to sacrifice our good for a greater good. What we want is very often not for our good! For self-centered creatures like us, it's often difficult to clearly distinguish what I want from what's good for me—and to go on keeping that distinction clearly in mind. But we have to stay in that mindset if we want to examine the question of whether God ever puts something else ahead of our good.

Once we do that, we'll be ready to look at a third thing to notice about this passage. It says "all things work together for good" for us. All things! For the almighty creator God, that covers a lot of ground. And it is not just that each thing, by itself, may serve our good in some way. God has orchestrated everything he ever made so that all the things that exist "work together" in a single, integrated plan to produce our good.

And lest we think "all things" in this passage may not really mean *all* things, but have some narrower reference, notice the context. What immediately precedes it? A discussion of how the curse has affected "the whole creation" (Rom. 8:22). And what immediately follows? A discussion of how "the love of God in Christ" for us supersedes "anything else in all creation" (Rom. 8:39). When Paul says all things work together for good for us, he means *all things*!

It's true, as Isaiah 48:11 reminds us, that God will not sacrifice his name or his glory to anything else. But it appears from passages like Romans 8:28 that this is not inconsistent with his arranging everything he ever made for the good of his people. It would appear that our good—our true good, as opposed to what we want—never comes into conflict with God's name or his glory. God doesn't have to prioritize between what is good for us and his own glory; they never come into competition.

And that shouldn't be surprising! God made us for himself, for fellowship with him. He created us so he could glorify himself by giving us our good, and we could glorify him by enjoying the good he gives us. And we are the pinnacle of creation, the image bearers who glorify God in a way that no majestic mountains or unfathomable ocean depths, no sublimely overwhelming galaxies and nebulae, even no angel or archangel ever could.

Hard as it may be for small and sinful creatures like us to believe, God redeems us and arranges everything in the universe for our good because *we are God's top priority.*

Why Only Some?

Unfortunately, most theological systems don't maintain this truth consistently. They think God puts something else ahead of us. And it's not God's name or his glory they put between us and God, but a created thing. Paul said that "neither death nor life, nor angels nor rulers, nor things present nor things to come, nor powers, nor height nor depth, nor anything else in all creation, will be able to separate us from the love of God in Christ Jesus our Lord" (Rom. 8:38–39). But most theological systems think there is something in the created order that God puts ahead of people, even those people who are his own people in Christ.

In fact, Calvinism is the only theological tradition that does not reach this conclusion. Just as Calvinists pull back from compromising the personal nature of God's saving love, they also pull back from compromising its supreme position in God's scheme of priorities for the created order. As we will see, those two issues are closely related.

The first thing we noticed about the promise that all things work together for good was that it was only for those who love God. We naturally want to ask, why is it only God's people who are God's top priority? Why don't all things work together for everyone's good? Does God make his own people his top priority, but not other people?

Just as we recoil from the idea that Jesus did his saving work for some people but not others, so we recoil from the idea that God designed the created order so that everything works together for the good of some people but not others. And we run into exactly the same problem we saw in the last chapter: God is all-powerful, yet some people are not saved.

We want to believe that God wants a universe where everyone is fully blessed. But we can't picture him trying to make such a universe and failing (because God is all-powerful), and we also can't picture him trying and succeeding (because not everyone is fully blessed). So we start looking around for some way to account for God's benevolence to us in the design of the universe that will not involve God either failing in his purpose or choosing to favor some but not others.

It's the same old theological snipe hunt, the diagram representing God's love as a square circle. And just as the attempt to assimilate the Son's work into this self-contradictory theological system led to the impossible supposition of a "hypothetical substitution," the attempt to assimilate the Father's work into it leads to similar impossibilities.

Nature over People

If God loves everyone in a way that would lead him to make everyone fully blessed, yet we aren't all fully blessed, there must be something else God loves that he values more highly than our blessedness. There must be something else that's a higher priority for God. And it wouldn't be enough to say that God's glory is a higher priority for him, because he can obviously glorify himself in many ways, including by saving us. So it must be something else in the created order that God values more than saving us, because that thing (whatever it is) glorifies God more.

That thing, according to all theological traditions besides Calvinism, is the general system of nature. I must immediately stop to clarify that "nature" here includes human nature and humanity's place in the larger natural order. Our ability to think, feel and act, our moral responsibility, and our dominion over the rest of nature are all part of the general system of nature that God created. Human free will is a natural phenomenon; it's part of the natural order.[2]

Other theological traditions say God gives higher priority to the general system of nature than he does to saving any particular individual person. God wants to save all people, but he will not save any person in a way that contravenes the natural order. Rather, he inserts a salvation system into the natural order and allows it to unfold within that order. He intervenes in nature—that is, in history, which is just the ongoing process of nature constantly unfolding itself in new events—not to save any particular person, but only to insert the salvation system. The salvation of any individual person is determined by whether the unfolding of the natural order causes him or her to get plugged into the salvation system.

As before, this view is most clearly visible in Roman theology. According to the Church of Rome, Jesus's work created the sacramental system. That was the intervention God was willing to make in nature to provide for salvation. Once he creates the system, he lets history—the unfolding of nature—continue with the sacramental system inside it. Who gets saved by the sacramental system is determined not by God's independent choice, but by who naturally comes to be plugged into the system and who doesn't. If the unfolding of nature, which includes your own choices and the choices of other people, causes you to be plugged into the system, you're saved. If not, you're not.[3]

The same view is at work, though less obviously, in Protestant traditions. In the Lutheran tradition, God equally values the salvation of all people, so he inserts the means of grace into history, then he steps back and lets history—that is, nature—take its course. (This was not Martin Luther's view, but that's a topic for another day.) The gospel, the most important means of grace, is not as directly tied to the corporate institutions of the visible church as the sacraments are. So superficially it appears that Lutheranism does not subordinate salvation to nature quite as much as Rome. In fact, it does. Who hears and believes the gospel is determined not by God's independent choice but by the general unfolding of events in nature.

In the Arminian traditions, God's preference for nature over our salvation is equally present, but even less obvious to the casual observer. In contrast to Lutheranism's ambiguity about the sacraments, Arminianism insists that salvation rests only on our response to the gospel. And most Arminians further hold that in the general system of nature, a supernatural work of the Holy Spirit in the heart is required before sinful people will believe the gospel. God values the salvation of all people, and to that end he inserts into history not only the gospel, but also the Holy Spirit to supernaturally draw us toward it. Here, it seems, God's saving love breaks through the chains of nature.

But in fact, it is not nature we are being freed from on this conception. It is only the corruption caused by original sin. Far from taking us out of nature, the Holy Spirit replaces one natural condition with another. He takes us from fallen nature to uncorrupted nature; he restores us to the natural condition of Adam in the garden. When the Spirit works, we have a natural ability to believe the gospel and a natural ability to disbelieve. The outcome is determined by our choice—in other words, by nature. If the unfolding of nature includes our choosing to disbelieve, God will maintain that natural outcome rather than contravene it.

Salvation Limited by Nature

All these views imply that God loves the natural system more than he loves any particular person. Just as the desire to say that the Son does his saving work for all people gives us a saving work that doesn't save, the desire to say that the Father's supreme love is directed to all people gives us a Father whose love for us is not supreme.

The insertion of the salvation system into nature is, certainly, a supernatural act. It transcends the natural order. So we can still say God loves the salvation of humanity in general—"humanity" in the abstract—more than nature in general. He was willing to contravene nature in order to create the salvation system.

However, on this view God is not willing to contravene the natural system in order to save any particular person. By creating the salvation system, he has given us much supernatural help toward reaching salvation. But when the chips are down, if the unfolding of the general system of nature is not going to get you plugged into the salvation system, God will choose to let you perish forever rather than contravene the natural system specifically to save you.

Here's another way of putting it. On this view, God loves us more than he loves fallen nature, nature as it stood immediately after the fall, with sin but without a salvation system. That's why he was willing to intervene in fallen nature on our behalf. However, he does not love us more than he loves nature as it stands after he inserts the salvation system. Once that system is installed, God loves nature more than us.

God created the salvation system because he "loves humanity" in the abstract, not because he loves particular people. Therefore, the salvation system ensures that "people"—somebody—will be saved. But God doesn't love any particular person enough to ensure *that person* will be saved. That's out of his hands.

So God does not choose which particular people are saved. He delegates that determination to the natural order, because he loves the natural order more than he loves any particular people. He "chooses" the saved and "chooses" the lost only in the sense that he chooses to leave them in the hands of nature and to abide by whatever choice nature makes.

A God Who Loves Systems More than People

Calvinists sometimes make the mistake of framing this exclusively as an issue of God's sovereignty, his all-powerful or "omnipotent" nature. They paint these other views as picturing a God who wants to save all people but is unable to do so because the system of nature stands in his way, forming a barrier to his will. Or else it's a picture of a God for whom our salvation is like one of those carnival games where you drop your ball in the top, then stand back and watch as it bounces down through a series of obstacles, waiting to find out whether it will drop into the "winner" hole or the "try again" hole. Each of us is one of those balls, and God just watches us as we bounce through life, finally dropping into either the "heaven" hole or the "hell" hole.

Indeed, some adherents of these views do talk that way. For example, Lewis writes explicitly that God compromised his omnipotence when he created creatures with free will.[4]

But the real error at the heart of these views is the idea that God loves systems more than he loves people. It's easy to formulate these theologies so that they don't compromise God's sovereignty. All you have to do is say that when God made the universe, saving people wasn't as important to him as preserving the system of nature.

We saw one aspect of this issue in the last chapter, where we confronted the choice between a Son who saves people and a Son who creates a salvation system. Now we confront the issue in its most general form—the choice between a Father who prioritizes systems and a Father who prioritizes people.

Priorities are about love. A Father who prioritizes systems above people is a Father who loves systems more than he loves people. He will even damn countless multitudes of people eternally—people whose salvation he values as highly as everyone else's—solely to protect the integrity of the system. He gave his only Son for us, but he loves the system of nature too much to sacrifice it for our sakes.

God's Unconditional Love

Over against all these conceptions, Calvinism says that God loves his people more than anything—certainly more than systems. Just as he loves human persons rather than "humanity," he loves human persons rather than "human nature." This is what Calvinists mean when they say God's love for his people is "unconditional." The usual explanation of this term is that God's love for us doesn't depend on anything in us. That's true, and it's very important. But the broader doctrine here is that God's love for us is independent not only of everything in us, but of everything whatsoever except God himself.

God loves you so much that he will utterly demolish all obstacles in order to save you. He will smash right through the system of nature—the orderly working of the whole creation, the system that holds together all the countless stars and planets and people and archangels, which he made at the beginning and pronounced "very good"—without a second thought, if that's what it takes to save you. In fact, it is, and he has.

He smashes right through even your own nature. Your nature, originally, hated God. So God didn't just fix some problems with your nature, then step back to see if your nature would accept him. He annihilated your love of sin. He killed your old heart and gave you a new heart that would love him instead. We'll look more extensively at this particular aspect of God's work in the next chapter.

Nature Is for Man, Not Man for Nature

Not only does God love people more than nature, but he also made nature in the first place only because he loves people. The whole system of nature is here because God wants us to have it. He wants us to use it, and he wants us to enjoy it (1 Tim. 6:17).

Those who think the Father puts systems ahead of people have got it all backward. God didn't create nature because he wanted to have systems. God created systems because he wanted nature to serve people's needs. God's love is personal; therefore people come first, nature second, systems third. So whenever any system is inadequate to accomplish his purposes for people, he just transcends it.

But if people didn't come first with God, if God's motive for saving us were that he "loves humanity" in the abstract, then it would make perfect sense that systems would come first. For that kind of God, abstract conceptual classifications of things (humanity) are more important than the concrete, individual things that make up those classifications (you and me). On that assumption, it makes perfect sense that he would create a salvation system rather than actually saving us, and that he would value the system more than he values any particular person's salvation.

Thankfully, the biblical God loves people more than abstractions. The more fully and deeply we absorb this truth—in other words, the more Calvinistic our piety becomes—the more fully and deeply we will love him back and have the joy of resting in God's personal love.

God Manifests His Justice

What about the lost? Does God love some people more than nature but not others? Does he refuse to save some people because he loves systems more than he loves those people? The answer is no. God's decision to pass over the lost and allow them to remain in their sins is just as "unconditional"—as independent of anything in creation—as his decision to save his people.

We have to distinguish between God's condemnation of the sins of the lost and his decision to pass them over for salvation. The condemnation, the judgment and punishment, are not unconditional. They are a response to something in the lost—namely, their sin. But that is not the reason God passes them over. We know this because we, whom he has chosen for salvation, are just as sinful as the lost. Even Paul calls himself "the foremost" among sinners (1 Tim. 1:15). If God's decision to pass people over for salvation were determined by their sin, he would pass everyone over and no one would be saved!

If the lost were passed over due to anything in them, then our salvation would be subordinate to the system of nature, just as much as if we were chosen to be saved due to anything in us. On that assumption, the saved would be saved not due to God's unconditional choice but because the general outworking of nature didn't cause them to have whatever it was in the lost that made God pass them over. So if the saved are saved due to God's unconditional choice, the lost must be lost due to the same choice.

God loves all people, even the lost, more than he loves mere systems. The Bible indicates that God intends to bless the lost. In Matthew 5:43–48, when Jesus tells us we should love and bless those who hate us, he justifies this by pointing out that we are called to imitate God—and God showers down blessings on those who love him and those who hate him alike.

But although God values the lost, there is something else he values more—his own name and glory as manifested in his justice. God prioritizes his justice over the salvation of the lost.

God is willing to extend mercy to some sinners, transferring their guilt and punishment to his Son out of love for them. But it appears that he is not willing to forgo the punishment of all sinners. He values his justice too much to permit that.

So while God always values people more than systems, "all things" do not "work together for good" to those whom God has not chosen for mercy. For these people, it appears that their good in the fullest sense—their total flourishing—does come into competition with God's glory. God's treatment of them is good, considered in itself, but it is not aimed at producing what would be their highest and fullest good as creatures, which would be fellowship with God.[5]

The Great Mystery

And now we come, at last, to the great mystery. If saving the lost is less important to God than manifesting his justice, why is saving us more important? If God's choice is unconditional, why did God choose us?

We know there must be a reason. God is not arbitrary and he does nothing at random. There is no chaos in God's universe, no mere chance. From the smallest events (Matt. 10:29–31) to the largest (Dan. 4:35), everything happens for a reason that is part of God's plan; so must this.

But we don't know what the reason is. If the reason doesn't lie in us—which it doesn't, because his choice is unconditional—then it must lie within himself. We know he is pleased to save some and not others, and we know he must have reasons. But his reasons are his own.

There is a very edifying Scripture in the book of Deuteronomy, when Moses is announcing the renewed covenant between God and his people at Moab. He says, "The secret things belong to the LORD our God, but the things that are revealed belong to us and to our children forever, that we may do all the words of this law" (Deut. 29:29).

This is a balance we must maintain. On the one hand, we must not speculate about the secret things God has not chosen to reveal to us. On the other hand, we must not deny or neglect any of the truth God has chosen to reveal. We must uphold that truth and pass it on to our children so that we may do all the words of God's covenant.

It pleases God to save you. It did not please God to save Judas. It has pleased him to reveal both of those facts to you and further to reveal that he has a reason for all he does, and his reason for saving you and not Judas has nothing to do with anything in either you or Judas. But it has not pleased him to reveal what that reason is.

God Is on the Hook

All Christian theologies agree that God chose a people for himself before the foundations of the world were laid. This is affirmed so often in Scripture (see for example Eph. 1:3–14) that there is no getting away from it. The disagreement is over the basis of this eternal choice. Calvinists think God chose his people simply because of unconditional love for them. All other traditions think he chose them because he foresaw that the outworking of natural events—history—would plug them into the salvation system.

The underlying concern that's driving all the other traditions here is to avoid saying that there are some people God could have saved but chose not to. To protect God from being held responsible for the crime of choosing some people over others, they hold that God doesn't really make an independent choice. He simply "chooses" the people whom he foresees being saved by the natural outworking of the salvation system. It's the system—our failure to choose God, our neighbor's failure to share the gospel, our parents' failure to baptize us, etc.—that's at fault if some people aren't saved.

But in addition to being false, this defense doesn't even work on its own terms. They hope to defend God by pointing to the natural outworking of the salvation system as the culprit. But the natural outworking of the system is either under God's control or it isn't—and whichever way you answer that question, God ends up responsible for the lost being lost.

If the natural outworking of the salvation system is under God's control, then the argument changes nothing. God doesn't independently control who is saved; he leaves it up to the system—that he controls. The issue of each person's salvation is still in God's hands. If anyone is lost, God is on the hook for that.

Yet how can we even say that God exercises no control over the system? God made the system. It exists in his universe. And God is all-powerful, in constant control of everything that happens in his universe. "I am God, and there is none like me, declaring the end from the beginning and from ancient times things not yet done, saying, 'My counsel shall stand, and I will accomplish all my purpose'" (Isa. 46:9–10). The universe wouldn't even continue to exist from moment to moment unless God were constantly upholding—in other words, controlling—it.

Never mind. Let's adopt for a moment the impossible supposition that God exercises no control over the system. How could God trust the eternal blessedness or cursedness of his precious image-bearing creatures to the whims of a system outside his control? How could he create people and then leave them at the mercy of a system that will make them eternally miserable—and do so not because he determined that the outcome was good, but for reasons of its own over which his good and perfect wisdom had (apparently) no control?

At the very least, God could have refrained from creating those whom he foresaw would be lost. No Christian would be prepared to say God was forced to create. That God created freely is a bedrock theological commitment; without it you get modalistic pantheism. So however unclear or confused our thoughts may be about how God treats the lost after creating them, we must at least agree that he was free not to create them at all. Why did he?

Jesus says it would have been better for Judas if he had never been born (Matt. 26:24). If God really values Judas's welfare as much as anyone else's, why was Judas born?

A Crime, Not an Accident

We don't want to picture God choosing to let some people remain lost when he could save them. However, this must be the case if God is the Creator of all things. And, hard as it is to accept, Scripture consistently testifies that the lost are lost because God passes them over (Prov. 16:4; Matt. 11:20–24; Rom. 9:1–29; 1 Pet. 2:8; Jude 4). The question is, Why does God prefer to condemn the lost when he could save them?

The assumption that God equally values the salvation of all people really comes from thinking of sin as a misfortune that has just happened to us, like a car accident. If a doctor arrived at the scene of a wreck and started picking and choosing which victims he preferred to save, that would be a terrible evil. When people are the victims of misfortune, we should help them without favor— because compassion is our duty to the victims of misfortune.

But sin is not a misfortune. It's something we do. It's a crime, not an accident. We need not only to be healed but also to be pardoned. In fact, it's crucial to the gospel of salvation through faith alone that the pardoning must come first and serve as the basis of the healing. Thinking that the healing came before the pardoning is exactly how the medieval church went off the rails; it's an open invitation to legalism.

As Calvinist theologian B. B. Warfield has put it, the proper analogy is not to a doctor healing the sick and wounded, but to a judge with a courtroom full of convicts he must sentence. A doctor must heal all those who come within reach of his care, but a judge is held back by higher considerations from pardoning every convict under his jurisdiction. It would be inexplicable if a doctor, having the power to cure all his patients, cured only some; but in the case of the judge, the wonder is not that he does not pardon all, but that he pardons any.[6]

God is not only a loving God but also a just God. And it appears that his justice is inconsistent with his pardoning all the criminals in his court. Like the judge who has a responsibility to uphold the law as well as to show mercy, God will not totally forgo the manifestation of his justice among sinners.

We trust in God not only because he loves us, but also because we know he is good—just, holy, and righteous. Personally, when I have difficulty accepting that God passes over some people for salvation, I try to turn those feelings in the direction of piety toward God's goodness. If it is horrible to me that some are lost, I begin by confessing to God that this very horror is the fate I deserved myself. Inevitably, the next thing I find myself doing is pouring out my heart in thankfulness that God chose to rescue me from that horror. Before long, I've become humble enough before God to rest in his goodness as well as his love.

I can do this not only because I know God is fully good and loving, but also because I know each person's standing with God is determined only by what pleases God's perfectly good and loving will for that person. Some are condemned because God is good. No one is ever condemned for the sake of a system.

3

God Loves You Irresistibly

*The "new birth" in the Holy Spirit is a
radical, supernatural transformation.*

Love that has to be earned isn't love. Our trust or our confidence we may rightly expect people to earn—even the people we love. The spouse who has lied may have to earn back our trust. The friend who has wasted money may have to earn our confidence before we make another loan. But love is not like that. If we expect people to earn our love, we're not really loving them at all. Love is a free gift; that's what makes it love.

Love doesn't even depend on the consent of the beloved. If someone you love tells you to stop loving him or her, do you? Of course not. You go on loving that person in another way.

When I was converted to Jesus, I lost one of my dearest friends in the world. This is a person whose wise counsel and generous friendship had been indispensible in seeing me through one of the darkest periods I ever went through. I believe I may owe her my life. And I know she treasured our friendship as well. However, she had built her own life around something that the Bible condemns, and now that I was a Christian I could not "be okay" with this central element of her life. I tried to handle the issue as gently as I could. But for her, simply knowing that I didn't approve of this part of her life was too much.

One day, she told me that in order to be true to who she was, she could never speak to me again. And she hasn't. That was about nine years ago.

I did not stop loving her. I pray for her every day—not just that God would draw her to himself in Christ, although of course I do pray for that, but also that God would bless her abundantly in her natural life. And, Lord willing and by his grace, I will keep on praying for her every day until the day I stop breathing.

When the people you love reject you, you go on loving them. Love does not depend on consent. If it did, it wouldn't be love. It would be a business deal—a contract.

On the other hand, we do need consent to be in a relationship. If someone we love rejects us persistently, the love doesn't end but the relationship is disrupted.

Often, out of selfishness, we refuse to acknowledge the rupture of a relationship. When this happens, what we call our "love" becomes merely a tool of our wicked possessiveness. Seeking reconciliation when our relationships are disrupted is of course perfectly legitimate. We can and should seek to persuade people to reconcile. But when we are denied an authentic restoration of the relationship by these legitimate means, we often seek a phony restoration by illegitimate means. We scream and threaten and bully, trying to force people back into relationship with us through domination; or else we beg and pander and grovel, trying to seduce our beloved into restoring the relationship by taking the dominant role.

In the face of persistent rejection, ordinate love accepts the rupture of the relationship. Of course it always remains open to restoration by legitimate means. But it accepts that without such a restoration, the relationship is ruptured. And then it goes on loving, just as intensely, in another way.

God Will Not Pretend

God's love for us involves this problem. He loves us, but we hate him. In the famous passage where Jesus tells Nicodemus that he came into the world because God loves the world, he immediately adds: "The light has come into the world, and people loved the darkness rather than the light because their works were evil. For everyone who does wicked things hates the light" (John 3:19–20). Even his own people return his love with hatred. He laments bitterly: "O Jerusalem, Jerusalem, the city that kills the prophets and stones those who are sent to it! How often would I have gathered your children together as a hen gathers her brood under her wings, and you would not!" (Matt. 23:37).

Of course, millions of people—inside the church as well as outside—think they love God when in fact they hate him. What they love is the tame "God" they've made up in their heads based on what they want God to be like. They keep the real God out of their consciousness. If they did become conscious of him, in all his holiness and power, they would hate him. (One proof of this is that they work so hard to keep him out of their consciousness!) To that extent, they hate him already. And this hatred is only a shadowy preview of the much more intensely hideous hatred for God that will ruin them throughout eternity, when they can no longer keep him out of their consciousness, unless they change before it's too late.

Because he is the perfect lover—indeed, because he is love—God goes on loving us in spite of our hatred. However, because his love is perfect, he will not pretend to be in fellowship with us while we hate him. From the first moments after the fall ("Where are you?" Gen. 3:9) to the present moment ("If we say we have fellowship with him while we walk in darkness, we lie and do not practice the truth," 1 John 1:6) to the consummation of all things ("Outside are the dogs and sorcerers and the sexually immoral and murderers and idolaters, and everyone who loves and practices falsehood," Rev. 22:15), God insists that we acknowledge our estrangement from him.

How does God handle this situation, where he loves us but is out of relationship with us because we hate him? Your answer will depend on what you think of the issues we looked at in the previous two chapters.

The Spirit as Persuader

Suppose you think God doesn't determine the outcome of our salvation on his own, but rather provides a salvation system and then lets us either get plugged into it or not get plugged into it. On this view, once God has created the salvation system, his only other job is to get us to use it. God has chosen not to transcend the natural order (other than to create the salvation system in the first place). So he must work on us within the natural order.

In short, God must persuade us. Just like us when we're confronted with rejection from those we love, God can—and does—seek to persuade us to reconcile. God must come to us and woo us. He must show us why we should take him back.

This is the role of the Holy Spirit in salvation, according to most theological traditions. First, the Holy Spirit suppresses our sinfulness just enough to make it possible for us—on our own—to naturally choose between accepting God or rejecting him. In some traditions this act is tied to baptism; in others it isn't. Then, in cooperation with the preaching of the gospel and other church ordinances, he coaxes and woos us to accept him. Without ever determining our choice, he uses inward, undetectable means to try to persuade us to move toward God.

In its essentials, the various non-Calvinist traditions differ very little on this point. The main differences concern how they relate the work of the Holy Spirit to the institutional church and (especially) the sacraments. For Rome, church and sacrament are essential; the Spirit does not ordinarily work apart from them. For Arminians, church and sacrament are still important but not essential; the gospel is the Spirit's only essential instrument. Lutherans occupy an ambiguous middle ground, with some gravitating toward one position and some toward the other.

But all these traditions agree that after the Holy Spirit has done his work, human nature—the natural system of our thinking, feeling, desiring, willing and so forth—is still in the driver's seat. Our salvation depends on how this natural system unfolds by itself, on its own. Through the Holy Spirit, God works to restore the natural system from the damage of original sin and to ensure that the system has favorable terms (persuasiveness) on which to operate. But in the end, the sinner must choose to repent and believe, or not, within the natural human system of thought, emotion, and desire rather than by divine action.

God will set you up, remove all obstacles *other than* your own voluntary turning away from him, and give you all the natural advantages he can. And then the key task—voluntarily turning toward God rather than away—is up to you, and only you. God stands by, awaiting your choice.

The Anxiety of Persuasion

This theology of the Spirit as persuader inevitably leads to an ecclesiology of the church as persuader. On the assumption that God is trying to persuade you to accept him, what determines how you will decide? Any number of factors, no doubt, but there is no avoiding the central role that must be played by the persuasiveness of the preacher and the church. If for no other reason, this is the factor with the most importance for ecclesiology simply because it's the only one that is under the church's control.

When the Holy Spirit's work is understood as persuasive, the human ministers who preach to us naturally believe that our eternal destinies depend on their ability (with God's help, of course) to persuade us to accept God. They are desperate to move us to consent to restore our relationship with God. They fear that if we don't, it will be their fault.

So they naturally project onto God all their anxiety to extract our consent. And since human preachers are only human, the anxiety frequently becomes dysfunctional—when legitimate reconciliation with God is denied, they seek illegitimate reconciliation. This is why so many sermons make God sound like a dysfunctional lover. God either seems to be bullying us into a relationship through domination, by threatening us with hell; or seducing us into a relationship through bribery, by offering fulfillment of our desires on self-oriented terms.

Let me hasten to add that this is all unintentional. Of course no one is encouraging this mind-set on purpose. Quite the opposite— all sensible observers seem to agree that there is a severe crisis in the state of preaching in the church today. And the same theologians who teach the Spirit-as-persuader model also insist that it is neither Paul nor Apollos, but God who gives the spiritual increase (1 Cor. 3:6).

Yet their insistence on this point does not much change the preaching on the ground. The anxiety to persuade continues to bubble up continually in regular preaching. That's because it is inherent in the theology that forms and guides that preaching. As long as they teach that the work of the Spirit is to persuade, there will be no essential change in the preaching informed by that model.

Theologians attempt to circumvent this problem by insisting that the persuasive power of the gospel is in the work of the Holy Spirit, not in the preacher. However, all they are really acknowledging is that the work of the Holy Spirit is necessary to conversion: without the Holy Spirit, the persuasion could not succeed. But while they believe it to be necessary, they do not believe it is sufficient. The central commitment that distinguishes their theology of the Spirit from Calvinism is precisely that the work of the Spirit is not sufficient to convert a sinner. And that is just where the anxiety of persuasion comes from. If something more than the Spirit's work is needed, how can the preacher not conclude that the quality of his work—his persuasiveness—is vital to the outcome?

Indeed, far from minimizing the anxiety of persuasion, most churches eagerly embrace "persuasiveness" as a model or standard by which their worship and evangelization should be judged. The job of the church is not to proclaim and embody the Word of God but to sell it.

Where authoritarian personalities predominate, the gospel is infected with a bullying spirit. In an evangelism ministry, I once saw a woman actually try to *trick* people into agreeing to hear a gospel presentation. I also saw the same woman run across a parking lot and grab people to try to extract an agreement to hear the gospel. She was just so worried that these people would go to hell if she didn't cram the gospel down their throats.

Where permissive personalities predominate, the gospel is infected with a seductive spirit. How often have we heard preaching about how faith will help you deal with your problems, clean up your emotional disturbances, mend your relationships, and in general fix up your life? Or help society reduce crime, end poverty, win wars, and in general fix up its life? Don't get me wrong—I think faith does, in fact, produce all sorts of wonderful blessings, including most of the ones that get preached about in these sermons. But is that why we should believe?[1]

I'm not trying to putt up one set of churches against another here. These deficiencies are as much present in Calvinist churches as in any others. In fact, both the bullying and the seductive examples I've just referenced above were drawn from my experience in Presbyterian churches—churches that were at least nominally Calvinist.

But I do believe that one of the root causes of these flaws is a conception of the Holy Spirit's work as persuasion. Since the Holy Spirit only restores and assists the natural mind and will, what this conception really boils down to is that we, the church, must be persuasive. So much is riding on the pastor's or the evangelist's persuasiveness!

The Arrogance of Choice

The flip side of the anxiety of persuasion is the arrogance of choice. When people are told that they determine their own eternal destinies, they can't help but picture God as coming to them, wooing them, asking for permission to work in their lives. This conception puts people in the driver's seat with God. That obviously creates difficulties getting people to conceive of God as a sovereign Lord.

It is a notorious fact—it is "scandalous" in the original sense of bringing shame and discredit on the gospel—that even in conservative Christian subcultures today, people's personal behavior is not much better than the world's. The defenders of Christianity during the Roman persecution constantly pointed to the superior virtue and diligent service to others that prevailed in Christian families. If we defended ourselves against persecutors that way today, we'd be laughed at.

Obviously the lordship of God doesn't exclude his love and even his friendship. We are supposed to call God "Abba," an intimate term for addressing a father (Rom. 8:15). Jesus calls himself our spiritual husband (for example, Matt. 9:15). And it is not for nothing that the Pharisees mocked Jesus by calling him "the friend of . . . sinners" (Matt. 11:19; Luke 7:34).

But God's desire for fatherhood, husbandhood, and friendship with sinners should be as humbling for us as it was offensive to the Pharisees. The casual "buddy Jesus" of so many churches today leaves no room for Jesus as lord and king.

This observation that we have a crisis of Jesus's lordship in the modern church is now so commonplace that it needs no elaboration. But some of the underlying causes are not always noticed.

Just as the theologians in non-Calvinist traditions acknowledge the principle of 1 Corinthians 3:6, so they also acknowledge that sinful human beings have no right to refuse God. On their view, the choice to believe or not to believe is "free" in the sense that God will not stop us from going whichever way we wish. But it is not "free" in the sense that either decision is equally okay, like the choice between vanilla or chocolate. Scripture describes the gospel as something that all people must "obey" (2 Thess. 1:8, 1 Pet. 4:17). Accordingly, theologians of all traditions agree in insisting that when Jesus urges us to believe, he is not just offering us a really good deal that we would be nuts to pass up. Jesus is Lord.

And yet, as with the anxiety of persuasion, the theologians' acknowledgments are ineffective because the underlying problem is in the theology itself. The plain fact is that they picture God offering us a deal. It may be a deal that we have a duty to accept, but it remains a deal. It's not even clear that we could call it a "covenant," since God's covenants don't seem to presuppose our consent—God didn't give Noah or Abraham or Moses a choice whether to accept his covenants. The gospel as conceived by non-Calvinist theology is a contract.

Nor does the arrogance of choice stop at the moment of conversion. Throughout your life, from moment to moment, you are always choosing either obedience to God or sin and rebellion. What determines which you choose? Again, the Holy Spirit may woo you and draw you toward God, but he will not change your will directly. When these traditions say God sanctifies you, they really mean that you sanctify yourself with God's help. The shocking conclusion is that for the entire span of your natural life and even through all eternity in heaven, you will only ever become as good and holy as God can persuade you to become.

Incidentally, the arrogance of choice also involves the anxiety of choice. Did I really give myself over to Jesus? Or am I self-deceived? I still sin. I know that sinful hearts are deceptive and above all self-deceptive. So how can I know I truly chose Jesus? When the ultimate issue of eternal life or death is determined by my own choice, there will always be this element of self-doubt. (We will treat the whole topic of the life of faith after conversion at much greater length in the next chapter. Also, on the assurance of salvation, see the appendix, question 11.)

A Miracle in Your Heart

Over against the theology of the Holy Spirit as persuader, Calvinism says the Holy Spirit works a miraculous supernatural transformation in us.[2] Confronted with a human nature that hates him, God does not just partially repair it and then see if he can get it to go the right way on its own. He obliterates the old nature's slavery to sin—he annihilates it entirely. God doesn't mess around with sin; he kills it.

Then he installs a new nature in us. The Calvinist doctrine is not antinatural. Human beings are designed to be natural creatures. God doesn't change us from human beings into angels. He changes us from human beings whose nature rejects God into human beings whose nature accepts God.

Among the many Scriptures teaching this, consider the episode after Jesus announces that only those who eat his flesh and drink his blood are truly in him, and only they will live. "When many of his disciples heard it, they said, 'This is a hard saying; who can listen to it?'" (John 6:60). This is the key question on which the whole issue turns. Who can "listen to," that is, who can accept, the gospel? How is it that the natural man, whose predispositions are all selfish, comes to turn away from his selfishness enough to believe the "hard sayings" of the gospel? Jesus answers: "It is the Spirit who gives life; the flesh is no help at all" (John 6:63). To make the issue absolutely clear, he adds: "This is why I told you that no one can come to me unless it is granted him by the Father" (John 6:65). Here we have the whole Trinity working together to transform the unbeliever into a believer—the Father "grants" that the Spirit will "give life" such that the person "comes to" the Son. The person obviously responds to this work by actively believing; otherwise he didn't come to the Son at all. But what does he contribute to the spiritual transformation that brought about his belief? "The flesh is no help at all."

Calvinism objects to the idea that God works our salvation entirely within nature and will not transcend it—that God limits himself to the limits of our nature. God's work does affect our natures. But it affects our natures by transcending our natures. God changes our natural systems of thinking, feeling, and willing not by working within the framework of our natural system, like a counselor, but by cutting out our natural system and transplanting a new one, like a surgeon.

The work of the Holy Spirit transcends our natures so completely that we're not even aware of it while it's happening. We become aware of it after the fact. This is what Jesus was pointing to when he said "The wind blows where it wishes, and you hear its sound, but you do not know where it comes from or where it goes. So it is with everyone who is born of the Spirit" (John 3:8). The Greek word for "Spirit" is the same as the word for "wind." We become aware of the Spirit only by detecting the evidence that the Spirit's work produces—"its sound"—after it has worked.

However, although the Spirit transcends my nature, this does not mean he actually annihilates me, the person, and creates a new person in my place. My slavery to sin is annihilated, but I am not. Even my sin, as such, is not yet annihilated; that will come later, after death. For now, I continue to have sin in myself, and as a result I still sin even after I'm transformed. But my enslavement to sin is gone.

And although the Spirit works a supernatural transformation in my heart, this does not mean the Spirit's work is completely unrelated to the natural events going on both outside me and inside me. That's how we know it's happening and how we understand what it is that's happening. If the supernatural work of the Spirit were totally disconnected from natural events, we would never know it had happened—to return to Jesus's metaphor, we would never "hear" the "sound" of the "wind." Of course, God could have chosen to save his people supernaturally without any connection to natural events if he had wanted to. But he chose not to. Even though the Spirit's core work miraculously transcends nature, God chose to save his people in ways that are intimately connected to nature. He wanted us to know what was going on.

Outside me, I hear God calling on me to repent and believe. I hear him through the Bible and the preachers of the gospel whom he has sent. The Bible specifically says that when pastors preach the gospel, God is using them to speak to people (Isa. 55:10–11; 2 Tim. 3:16–17; 1 Pet. 4:11). These are natural events God has chosen to use as instruments of his supernatural work. He sometimes works without them—for example, on the road to Damascus, Jesus preached the gospel to Saul directly through a supernatural event. The Bible also indicates that God sometimes works this transformation in infants, which obviously means he can do it without an exterior preaching of the gospel at all (we'll return to that topic below). But he normally uses natural events to preach the gospel to people as a prelude to the Spirit's work. Apparently, it glorifies God to use human gospel preaching as the primary backdrop or setup that prepares us to know and understand the imperceptible miracles being secretly worked in our hearts.

Inside me, I respond to the Spirit's work. And I am no puppet—my response is the spontaneous and authentic response of a human being with free will who has been miraculously liberated from slavery to sin. I become aware of Jesus's saving work, and I put my trust in him. I abandon all hope that my own works can contribute to my right standing with God. And I resolve to turn away from sin and never again be content with my own sinfulness, to spend the rest of my life sincerely striving to love and serve God and my neighbor, as far as God's enabling grace permits me to do so. This change of mind, heart, and will is what we're talking about when we talk about things like "making a decision for Christ." Different people experience the change differently—some all at once in a dramatic emotional cataclysm, and some so gradually, perhaps over the course of years, that they hardly know what's really happening to them. But this decision or change of will for Christ is imperative. This is what it means to be converted; it is the second birth without which no one can even see the kingdom of God. These are also natural events God has chosen to use. His supernatural work changes nature—specifically, it changes my nature—and therefore it produces natural results. My heart of stone has been miraculously removed and replaced with a heart of flesh; it's only natural that I'd be a very different person after such a transformation.

The key point here is that God can use these natural events without being dependent on them. Jesus used water to make miraculous wine; he used a few loaves and fish to make many loaves and fish. On these occasions he works miraculously to transcend the system of nature (water does not naturally become wine while contained in a jar) but remains intimately connected to nature (water does naturally become wine while contained in the fibers of a grape). By doing works that parallel or imitate the ordinary workings of nature, but clearly transcend them, he showed that he was above nature but not hostile to it—he was the Lord of nature, not its enemy. However, it would be ridiculous to think that Jesus was therefore dependent on these things—that he couldn't have provided wine if he hadn't had some water to start with. That is the whole point of Satan's tempting Jesus to make stones into bread; he can, in fact, turn stones into bread, but he chooses not to because it isn't the Father's will. Similarly, the Spirit saves me by transcending my nature (including my hearing of the gospel and my response to it) while remaining in intimate contact with it. In doing so he shows that he is the Lord of my nature, not its enemy. But if I thought his work was therefore dependent on my nature, I would be mistaken.

You Are a New Creation
By this supernatural transformation, we are miraculously liberated from our freely chosen slavery to sin. We are transformed from creatures whose spiritual nature rejects God into creatures whose spiritual nature accepts God. Notice that I said our natural slavery to sin is freely chosen and voluntary. As long as we are in our old nature, we *want* to be slaves to sin. That is why the God-as-persuader model doesn't work.

Earlier, I wrote that those who hold the God-as-persuader model believe the Holy Spirit removes all obstacles to our accepting God *other than* our own voluntary turning away from him. That conception is the root of the problem. There have never been—there never could be—any obstacles at all to our accepting God other than our own voluntary turning away from him. Our voluntary turning away from God is precisely the problem of sin. If God doesn't take away our voluntary turning away from him, then by definition God doesn't remove our sin.

What lies behind the God-as-persuader model is the conception of sin as a misfortune, something that happens to us rather than something we do. In the last chapter, we saw how this thinking lies behind the idea that God must value the salvation of all people equally. It lies just as much behind the idea that God restores our relationship without transcending our natures.

If only—goes this thinking—if only the sinner didn't have these burdens and barriers that keep him from God, he would be able to make a real choice. If only we didn't have these disordered *desires* pulling us away from God, if only we didn't have these sinful *thought patterns* hardening us against God, if only we didn't have all these *things*—these things that happen to us—that make it so hard, so very hard, to choose God. If only we weren't so unfortunate as to have these awful things happening to us!

It's all an illusion. The disordered desires and thought patterns are not something that cause sin. They are sin. God says wrong desires are sin (Matt. 5:28). God says wrong thought patterns are sin (Mark 7:21). As soon as Adam and Eve really *wanted* to eat the fruit God told them not to eat, they had already fallen.

Once we see that all these spiritual burdens are crimes we commit rather than misfortunes we merely labor under, it becomes clear that salvation is impossible without a radical (literally "at the root") transformation of our whole selves. The will is not something that needs to be liberated from something external to itself, namely these sinful desires and thought patterns. The desires and thought patterns are the will itself in action. Even though it doesn't feel like we choose them, their origin is always the disorder of our sinful will. Insofar as God truly takes away sinful phenomena from the human heart, he is taking away the sinful will. Rather than liberating the will from encumbrances, he is removing it entirely.

Think of it this way: If these desires and thought patterns were not manifestations of an anti-God will, why would they be bad?

Why is God offended by them? Why does he demand we work diligently to remove them? God is not a Pharisee or some sort of Victorian prude. That's not what his law is for. What God cares about is whether our hearts—and consequently all the rest of us—love him or hate him. Our desires and thought patterns wouldn't offend him if they didn't spring from a fundamentally anti-God will.

The heart is not a neutral nut surrounded by a sinful shell. It's an onion—peel away all the layers of sin and there's nothing left. This emptying out or taking away of the sinful will is exactly what needs to happen. It's not just the outer layers that need to be peeled away; the onion is rotten all through. God takes the whole smelly, repulsive vegetable and drops it in the garbage. Then he replaces it with a chocolate cake. (You health enthusiasts can substitute "fresh-cut carrot sticks" or something like that here.)

God says that when the Holy Spirit transforms us, we become "a new creation" (2 Cor. 5:17; Gal. 6:15). He promises to remove our sin-loving hearts of stone and give us God-loving hearts of flesh (Ezek. 11:19 and 36:26). He says that we were dead before he transformed us, but he raised us from the dead to have a new life in Christ (Eph. 2:5; Col. 2:13) so that in the end we can stand before Christ as he says, "Behold, I am making all things new" (Rev. 21:5).

When he says these things, he really means them. You are not a recovering sinner. You are a new creation.

God Does Not Use Force
People often object to this view of the Holy Spirit's work on grounds that it violates the moral rule that you must acknowledge the rupture of a relationship. They think the Calvinist view portrays God as a bully who forces himself on people who don't want him. When the Calvinistic view is compared with the God-as-persuader model, which portrays God as wooing and courting the soul, it is widely compared to rape. God demands that we accept him and will force us to do so.

This is a mere confusion. There is no similarity at all between the domineering actions of a bully and the supernatural transformation of the heart worked by God out of his selfless compassion. God does not threaten; God does not yell; God does not manipulate. Above all, God does not use violence. There is no violent force at all in the work of the Holy Spirit.

The Holy Spirit does not conquer, overpower, capture, or in any other way domineer over the resistance of the old nature. The reason is simple: the Holy Spirit does not even *encounter* the resistance of the old nature. There is no conflict, no struggle. The fundamental orientation toward sin in the old nature just vanishes—instantaneously annihilated.

In fact, the reason God miraculously transforms us is precisely because he upholds the moral law that a relationship requires consent. God desires fellowship with us, but we do not consent because we freely choose to be slaves to sin. And God will not seek fellowship with us as long as we remain that way. So, out of loving compassion, he miraculously rescues us from our freely chosen slavery to sin. As a result, we now genuinely desire reconciliation with the God we have rejected, and he takes us back into fellowship with him. God's moral design for relationships—love achieving fruition in voluntary (consensual) fellowship—is not undermined by the Spirit's supernatural action but rather restored.

God Transcends His Own Rules—Without Breaking Them

The key insight to grasp here is that God transcends his moral rules without violating them. That may sound like double-talk or splitting hairs. But it's an essential principle for all Christian theology.

If God couldn't transcend a moral rule without breaking it, there could be no atonement. One of the most fundamental of all moral rules is that God will never acquit the guilty (Ex. 34:7). We, of course, are all guilty—heinously so. That God will never acquit the guilty is a moral rule, so God will never break it. If it were not possible to transcend the rule without breaking it, we would have no hope.

Transcending this rule without breaking it is precisely what the atonement does. God looks at us and sees that we're guilty. He wants to acquit us, and he knows that he can never acquit the guilty. So, by an unthinkable miracle beyond all human understanding, he supernaturally transfers our guilt to Jesus and Jesus's righteousness to us. In this exchange, Jesus doesn't just take our punishment, he takes our guilt; in fact, the only reason he takes our punishment is because he takes our guilt. "For our sake he made him to be sin who knew no sin, so that in him we might become the righteousness of God" (2 Cor. 5:21). "He himself bore our sins in his body on the tree, that we might die to sin and live to righteousness" (1 Pet. 2:24). In punishing the guilty (Jesus) and rewarding the righteous (us), God is following out his own moral system. The system has been transcended but remains intact; the only thing that has changed is the identities of the guilty and innocent parties. There is a moral rule against acquitting a guilty person. But there is no moral rule against transferring that person's guilt to someone else and *then* acquitting him!

The Church of Rome objects to this doctrine, at least in the form in which Protestants have classically expressed it—that we become righteous solely because God declares us righteous. Rome says this makes our righteousness a "legal fiction." But it isn't a legal fiction; it's a legal fact, because God can change reality simply by declaring the change. (If you doubt it, check out Genesis 1.) When God declares you righteous, *you miraculously become righteous* simply because he declared it. Even when you continue to commit sins, you remain righteous because the righteousness of Christ has been judicially imputed to you by the gob-smackingly inexplicable working of God's power.

Now, if God can supernaturally make guilty people righteous and righteous people guilty without violating his own moral law against acquitting the guilty or condemning the righteous, he can certainly supernaturally replace our anti-God nature with a pro-God nature without violating his own moral rule against forcing yourself on people without their consent. Rather than work against our will, God simply replaces it. It's just like replacing our guilt with righteousness rather than acquitting us in spite of our guilt.

There are deep and profound parallels between the Calvinist views of the work of the Father, the Son, and the Holy Spirit. The Son actually saves us in the cross and the empty tomb, rather than merely making salvation possible. The Father actually chooses us, rather than merely ensuring that some people will be saved and leaving it up to nature to determine which ones. And the Holy Spirit actually removes our sin—our voluntary turning away from God—rather than merely suppressing or reducing its influence in order to make choosing God possible.

And, in fact, the three accounts all go together, hand in glove. In order to avoid saying that God values the salvation of some more than the salvation of others, all traditions except Calvinism are inexorably driven to say that God the Father loves nature more than people; that God the Son died and rose again not to save people but to create a salvation system within nature; and that God the Holy Spirit works on us within the limits of nature to persuade us to be saved. Because Calvinism is willing to accept the difficult fact that God values the salvation of some more than others, it can preserve the pure biblical truth that God the Father loves people (all people) more than nature; that God the Son actually saved us when he died and rose again; and that the Holy Spirit actually removes our sinful unbelief and restores us to fellowship with God.

Missing the Metaphors

When it comes to the work of the Spirit, I'm convinced that the popular misunderstanding of Calvinism arises largely because we tend to think about the Spirit's work only through the metaphor of Christ as our spiritual husband and the church as his spiritual bride. This exclusive focus on Christ's husbandhood makes it easy to erroneously conclude that the Calvinist view is analogous to rape while the other views are analogous to wooing or courting.

God uses metaphors to tell us about himself. That seems to be the only way God's attributes can be presented to our limited minds in a way we can grasp. Christ as our husband and the church as his bride is one of the more frequent and important metaphors, but there are many others. The names of the Father and the Son, for example, are far more common and more important in Scripture than the image of Christ's husbandhood, and those names are entirely metaphorical. God depicts the first two persons of the Trinity as Father and Son so that we can grasp something centrally important about their relationship. And this metaphor of fatherhood and sonship is applied to us as well, through its extension to concepts like adoption and inheritance (Rom. 8:14–17; 1 John 3:1–2).

No metaphor can perfectly capture the underlying reality that it exists to communicate. If it could, it wouldn't be a metaphor at all. We call an image metaphorical because it is similar to the underlying reality in some important way but not in all ways.

This makes it absolutely essential that we never allow only one of the biblical metaphors to inform our thinking about God. Each metaphor exists to show us some aspect of the divine perfection. We are given many metaphors so that we can grasp many aspects of that perfection. If we obsessively focus on one metaphor, we get only part of what God wants us to know about himself—and that can't help but distort our thinking.

That having been said, it is not difficult to construct an illustration that expresses how the Calvinist understanding of the Holy Spirit's work can be integrated with the biblical metaphor of Jesus as our spiritual husband and ourselves as his spiritual bride.

His Love Is Stronger than Our Hate

Once upon a time, a young man met a young woman, and the two of them fell in love. After a giddy and exciting courtship, brimming with anticipation, the young man resolved to ask the young woman to marry him. He spoke to her father, acquired the ring, planned out the most romantic possible setting for the proposal, and invited her to meet him there.

Now the young woman studied chemistry. Being intelligent and spirited, she was of a curious nature. On the morning of the day on which the young man was planning to propose marriage, she was visiting a pharmaceutical plant to learn about its processes. Succumbing to temptation, she tampered with the machines in her desire to learn more about them, and she was exposed to a toxic chemical. She was immediately thrown into a state of deranged madness. She hated everyone in the world, most especially the young man who loved her.

Later that day, when the young man asked her, "Will you marry me?" she denounced him in a rage of cursing and swearing such as no one in that town had ever heard. She was brought in for treatment, but the doctors couldn't help her. They pronounced her condition irreversible and untreatable.

Her madness grew worse, until she would physically attack anyone who even approached her. Before long she was confined to an asylum, kept in restraints at all times. There she lay for years and years, strapped to her gurney, endlessly raging and cursing against the world.

Now the young man was like the young woman, intelligent and spirited. He dropped out of law school to study medicine, becoming a doctor. Working night and day for years, at long last he discovered a way to cure her condition.

From the instant he entered her cell, she screamed imprecations at him more horrible than any she had uttered in all her long years of madness. When they removed her arm restraint to administer the injection, she seized the front of his throat and plunged her fingernails in as deeply as she could. In her insanity, she wanted to tear out his larynx and eat it. The orderlies pulled her arm away, but his five wounds were deep, and they never fully healed.

As he administered the injection, she began screaming "No!" over and over. She continued screaming it after he left, until she had screamed it 666 times. But the treatment worked, and when she woke up the next day, she came to herself. When he walked into her cell to see how it was with her, she cried out "Yes!" They wept. As they embraced, she began saying "Yes!" over and over, until she had said it seven times seventy times.

He nursed her back to health, their amazing story spread to international fame, and they were at long last married in a ceremony that captured the attention of the entire world. When the minister had pronounced them man and wife, the husband leaned in to kiss her, and she whispered, "Thank you that your love was stronger than my hate."

Conversion Is the Engagement, Not the Wedding

As I said, no metaphor perfectly captures the underlying reality. Most importantly, in this story a mental illness serves as the analogue to sin. That is not a perfect analogy because mental illness is not a moral failure. But there is nothing in our human experience that strictly corresponds to the Holy Spirit's miraculously liberating us from our voluntary slavery to sin. I chose the curing of a mental illness as the closest thing I could find.

Also, in this story there is an element of restraining the bride and overcoming her resistance by force. That is inevitable if we tell it as a story about human beings because human beings can't just miraculously change reality the way God can. I tried to make it clear that the physical restraint was only tangentially related to the central drama—the curing of her illness.

The central point is that the woman does not go from "no" to "yes" because the man persuades her, or even because of any form of interaction at all with him. What was needed was a change in her nature. He does not threaten, bully, cajole, or plead with her. He transforms her—even against her will.

An additional point: in the biblical analogy between salvation and the husband/wife relationship, the moment when a person accepts Jesus does not correspond to the wedding night. It corresponds to the engagement. The marriage of the Lamb takes place at the end of history (Rev. 19:6–10). And God forbid that we should think our spiritual lover has any desire to proceed to the wedding night before the marriage takes place! In this, as in so many other

111

ways, his love is not like our love. His desire for his beloved is more intense than that of any merely human bridegroom, but he is also the consummate gentleman.

People think the God-as-persuader model corresponds to courtship and that Calvinism corresponds to rape because they neglect this point. In fact, precisely because the Spirit's work is a miraculous transformation, there is really nothing in our natural human love that corresponds to the work of the Holy Spirit in regenerating us. That's why I had to invent something else besides the romantic relationship—the mental illness and the cure—in order to tell the story.

And the process of courtship or "wooing" that precedes an actual marriage proposal does not correspond to anything in our relationship with God. In human relationships, you court first, then you propose marriage. That's because the purpose of courtship is to figure out whether you ought to get married. But God is not trying to figure out whether you and he are right for each other.

On the other hand, the process of courtship that takes place in conjunction with, or after, the actual marriage proposal is very much analogous to our relationship with God. In a sense, God's courtship begins with the proposal. And as any married person can tell you, the courtship that takes place after you've entered into the marriage covenant is a completely different sort of thing from the courtship that takes place before.

"Set Open unto All Men"

Some of you want to object: all this talk about how the Holy Spirit removes the sin of those God has chosen to save may be very inspiring. But what about the lost? What does Calvinism say God does about them?

In those cases, God simply accepts the rupture of the relationship. He allows people who freely choose to be out of fellowship with him to remain that way forever—with all that entails. This often seems cruel to us because in our own relationships we always wish to be open to legitimate reconciliation. The Calvinist doctrine seems to give us a God who doesn't want to be reconciled to some of his creatures.

In fact, God says he's open to reconciliation with anyone who wishes it. "Ask and it will be given to you; seek, and you will find; knock, and it will be opened to you. For everyone who asks receives, and the one who seeks finds, and to the one who knocks it will be opened" (Matt. 7:7–8). "As I live, declares the Lord GOD, I have no pleasure in the death of the wicked, but that the wicked turn from his way and live; turn back, turn back from your evil ways, for why will you die, O house of Israel?" (Ezek. 33:11).

Calvinists have always acknowledged and celebrated this truth. "No man is excluded from calling upon God," Calvin writes. "The gate of salvation is set open unto all men; neither is there any other thing that keeps us back from entering in, save only our own unbelief."[3]

The key point is, although God is open to reconciliation, no one wants to be reconciled to God. As Paul's collection of Scriptures in Romans 3:10–18 makes clear, we're sinners who always freely and voluntarily choose to reject reconciliation. God doesn't tell us he's open to reconciliation with anyone because he hopes that it will happen. He knows it won't. He tells us because he wants it to be clear to everyone that the disruption of the relationship comes entirely from our side, not his. If anyone is out of fellowship with God, it's because he chooses to be.

Our disruption of our relationship with God is not like the disruption of human relationships. With other people, there is always some hope for reconciliation. But our hatred for God leaves no room for such hope. We hate God by our sinful nature. No amount of persuasion will ever change our minds. No matter how favorable the circumstances we create, no matter how winsome the arguments or how empathic the address, as long as we have a free choice we will always freely choose against God. That's just the kind of people we are.

God declares that he is open to reconciliation so it will be clear that it is us, not him, who disrupt the relationship. But he is no fool. He will not pretend that we may someday turn to him when he knows very well that we won't. We will always, always freely choose not to.

With those he has not chosen to save, God does precisely what a good human being does when faced with rejection from a loved one. He accepts that without legitimate reconciliation the relationship is disrupted. He declares himself open to reconciliation with all who seek it. But in the case of those he has not chosen, he knows with certainty that legitimate reconciliation will never come, because in their sinfulness, they will never seek him. They will always freely choose to reject him.

We Can't Have It Both Ways

The assertion that we will never consent to God unless our nature is transcended and replaced—that our natural resistance to God is implacable—is one of the most unpopular teachings of Calvinism. Yet this view cannot be separated from the idea that the work of the Holy Spirit is a fundamentally miraculous act. If we are capable of turning to God on our own, within our natural system of thinking, feeling, and willing, then clearly the job of the Holy Spirit is to get us to do just this. The conversion of a sinner is not a miracle but a natural act. On the other hand, if the Holy Spirit is miraculously transcending our natural system of thinking, feeling, and willing, this can only be because our natural system had to be transcended before we could be converted.

To avoid naturalizing the work of the Holy Spirit, traditions that embrace the God-as-persuader model emphasize other aspects of the Spirit's work that they hold to be supernatural. For example, some of them agree with Calvinism that fallen human beings are by nature implacably anti-God, but the Holy Spirit miraculously alleviates the influence of the fall just enough to restore the possibility of a voluntary repentance. The Spirit doesn't change the will itself directly but removes a bad influence or power that damages the will.

However, while this view allows some aspects of the Spirit's work to be supernatural, at bottom the core mission of the Spirit is persuading the natural will to turn to God. And persuasion of a natural will is a natural activity. If the Spirit's most central and fundamental work were supernatural, it could not be persuasion. It would be transformation—just what Calvinism says it is.

You can have a Holy Spirit who makes you a new creation by working miracles in your heart. Or you can have a human nature that is not implacably anti-God. You cannot have both. And Scripture persistently teaches both that our nature is implacably anti-God and that the work of the Holy Spirit is a radical, miraculous transformation.

We can't have it both ways. The human will in its natural state, before God works on it, is either capable of turning to God or it is not. If it is, then historic Christianity is false—that was the whole point of the early church's struggle against the legalizing heresy of Pelagianism. If it is not, then a radical supernatural transformation is needed. You can picture the Holy Spirit doing all the supernatural work you want on other parts of the human being, and all the natural persuading you want on the will itself, but as long as the natural will is not transformed, the sinner will not repent. And if you picture the Holy Spirit doing supernatural work to remove the sinner's natural, implacable rejection of God, you are really picturing him removing the old will entirely and implanting a new one—because the sinner's turning away from God is not something separate from his will; it is his will in action.

Renovated or Re-created?

The Calvinist view that the work of the Holy Spirit is miraculously transformational makes a dramatic difference in our devotional lives. All Christians fall on their knees and say to God, "You have made me a new creation!" But if our thinking falls short of the full biblical view of the Spirit's work—as it usually does among all us fallen sinners, regardless of our theology—we are saying this with an implied reservation. Often we only mean, "You have helped me to remake myself." But those are our worst moments. The real test is what we mean in our best moments. And unfortunately, I'm afraid that in our best moments we still only mean, "You have remade the part of me that resisted you—the part of me that needed remaking." If we really mean this, we shouldn't call ourselves new creations; we are renovated, not re-created. Whereas if we say, truly without reservation, "You have made me a new creation!" we are expressing the Calvinistic view.

Obviously this difference goes right to the heart of our primary problem as sinners: self-trust. The view of the Holy Spirit as persuader or renovator fails to fully empty us of our trust in ourselves, because all the work we attribute to the Holy Spirit is understood to be limited by our own permission. If the Holy Spirit does just as much work on me as I permit him to do, I cannot avoid the implication that I share some credit for the work, having been good enough to permit him to do it. Only when we stop seeing the Holy Spirit as a renovator and start seeing him as a re-creator can we really attribute all the efficacy of salvation to God alone.

The Calvinist view also provides the only secure comfort when we grieve for the spiritual state of our loved ones. Only Calvinism gives us a Holy Spirit capable of saving literally any person, so only the Calvinist can pray for the conversion of a loved one with the confidence that God really has the power to grant that prayer. More importantly, only Calvinism gives us a good Father who is in full control of the salvation process from beginning to end. Thus only the Calvinist has confidence that the final result of a loved one's spiritual journey will be the result that glorifies God the most. Indeed, the Calvinist knows not only that the end will be the one that most glorifies God, but even that the (often discouraging) spiritual journey itself is proceeding according to God's plan in the way that God has determined will glorify himself the most.

Entrusting Our Children to God

This last subject calls for some plain speaking. I have seen adherents of other theological traditions taunting Calvinists about the eternal fate of their children who don't profess faith. Do you, they ask, think God condemned your child to hell before she was even born?

How completely they misunderstand! I have confronted serious questions about the eternal fate of two children and gone through all the anguish that entails. So I can testify that from where I sit, Calvinism is the only real comfort. Don't get me wrong; I don't believe in Calvinism because I found comfort in it—I was a Calvinist long before we conceived our first child—but when I found comfort, I found it only because I believed in Calvinism.

My wife and I lost our first child to miscarriage. The Bible tells us God can save infants (2 Sam. 12:22–23; Ps. 22:9; Matt. 21:16; Luke 1:41–44). I don't know what I would think of that if I weren't a Calvinist. Obviously my child was in no position to make a decision for Christ, much less receive the sacraments, before birth. But being a Calvinist, I know that the Holy Spirit saves us by miraculously transforming us—which, of course, he can do to us at any age and in any state of development, since the transformation doesn't depend on anything we contribute. So I can prayerfully hope my first child is saved, and I can know with certainty that the issue will be decided in whatever way most glorifies a perfectly good God.

When Jesus angrily rebuked those who would stand between him and the "little children" (Greek scholars say the term refers to infants and small toddlers) and commanded that they be brought to him for blessing, the little children didn't come to Jesus of their own power. They were brought to him (Matt. 19:13–15; Mark 10:13–16; Luke 18:15–17).

That, of course, is not what the adherents of other traditions have in mind when they ask us about our children. They want to know what we think about our grown children who actively reject God. I've had experience with that, too.

When Anya, our second child, was four, she began articulating an intense hatred for God. "I don't love God! I hate God!" she would say whenever the subject came up. Told that God loved her, she would insist, "No, God doesn't love us!" She would say the same about Jesus. And she was not just seeking an excuse not to go to church; she genuinely thought God was her enemy.

You can imagine what we went through—the prayers, the anxiety, the anger, the fear. At one point I felt like I was walking around with a bowling ball in my stomach. And then one day—more suddenly than I would have thought possible—I found peace.

I don't know why, but for some reason I asked myself what I would say at Anya's funeral if she died that day, cursing God. Mentally reviewing the people who would be at the service—my family, my wife's family, my coworkers and friends, and my church family—I imagined myself standing there in front of a room full of non-Christians, Roman Catholics, evangelicals and Protestants of every description, and fellow Calvinists. How would I express what I believed?

Here's part of the speech that I wrote for myself in my head, as best as I can now reproduce it:

Yes, Anya hated God. And so do I.

So do we all. In this fallen world, to be a human being is to hate God. That's because God is good, and we're not. The Bible says all human beings other than Jesus are sinners. And part of being a sinner is hating God. Think about your sins. Rest assured, you have sinned today. You sin every day. You have sinned this very hour. And the Bible says that to sin is to hate God.

That's what makes God's love so amazing. He loves us even though we hate him. And he loves us so much that he saves us from the worst thing in the world, which is our hatred of him, and his perfectly good justice responding to our hate. That's what Jesus came here to do. He died on the cross and rose from the dead so that sinful people who hate God, like me, and like you, and like Anya, could be saved from hating God and from the eternal misery that such hatred obviously implies.

And God can save us no matter how much we hate him because the Holy Spirit has the miraculous power to transform our hearts. God doesn't need Anya's permission to save her. God can save Anya even if she hates him. He saved me without asking my permission. He didn't wait for me to love him before he saved me—just the opposite, he saved me because I didn't love him; he saved me so that I would come to love him, because I was miraculously changed. That's why God can save Anya as well. The Bible says God sometimes saves even infants, who can't think about him at all, much less love him or give him permission to save them.

I don't want to give anyone the wrong impression. When God saves us, he changes our hearts so that we love him. The hatred of God doesn't completely go away, but it is outmatched by the love of God that God himself gives us. So this is no excuse for anyone to just keep on sinning. And we're saved through faith in Jesus and only through faith in Jesus. If anyone here isn't trusting in Jesus alone for your standing with God, I would encourage you to learn more about Jesus's saving work and to talk to someone here in the church about him.

But the faith that saves us is a great mystery, existing—as we are told it sometimes can—in the heart of a child too small to even think. If God could give that faith to an unborn child, or to Paul, who called himself the foremost of sinners, then he can give it to Anya, too. He could very easily have done that for her before she died, and we'd know nothing about it. The Bible says that the Holy Spirit is like the wind, which blows where it wills, and you can't see it.

I believe God wanted us to hear our daughter saying she hated God. I think he had a very good reason. I think he wanted us to remember that we couldn't save her. We were called to take good care of her and teach her about God and encourage her in godliness, of course. But nothing we could do would save her. Only God can save. I think God wanted us to remember that. And I think he also wanted us to remember that we, ourselves, were also saved through no doing of our own, by God's grace, in spite of our hatred of him.

I'm very relieved to report that things are now well with Anya. She loves God and knows that God loves her. But by the time it had become clear that Anya no longer hated God, I had already found peace about Anya's fate by accepting that it was in God's hands, not ours or hers—because people who say "I hate God!" are exactly the kind of people God saves.

4

God Loves You Unbreakably

*You can do all things, persevere through all
trials, and rejoice in all circumstances.*

So far we've looked at three basic things about real love: it's personal, it's about setting priorities, and it doesn't have to be earned. These three things, taken together, imply one more thing: the essence of love is a willingness to endure suffering.

In chapter 1, looking at the role of the Son in our salvation, I wrote that real love isn't a feeling; it's a way of behaving. But we tend to prefer the feeling over the behavior because the behavior is often difficult, burdensome, and frustrating. In other words, real love involves self-sacrifice—a willingness to suffer. The Son gave us the ultimate example of that kind of sacrificial love on the cross. Anyone can *feel like* he loves other people, but what kind of love does it take to climb up on a cross and be tortured to death for them—even as they mock and jeer at you?

In chapter 2, looking at the role of the Father in our salvation, I wrote that real love is about setting priorities. The more you love something, the more you'll be willing to give up other things for its sake—that's how you know you love it so much. In fact, that's exactly what it means to say you love it so much. So the more you love something, the more painful sacrifices—suffering—it usually requires. The Father gave us the ultimate example of that kind of sacrificial love by giving up his Son for us. We often think about what the cross was like for Jesus; we can never really have more than a tiny glimpse of that experience, but Scripture does invite us to meditate on that glimpse, and we often do. Yet Scripture also invites us to meditate on what the cross was like for the Father, and we don't do that so much. Among other passages, consider what God says to Abraham about the offering of Isaac. "Take your son, your only son Isaac, whom you love, and go to the land of Moriah, and offer him there as a burnt offering" (Gen. 22:2). "Now I know that you fear God, seeing you have not withheld your son, your only son, from me" (Gen. 22:12). Listen to those words: offer up your son, your only son, your son whom you love. That's the voice of a Father who knows what it's like to give up a beloved Son. How much must he love us to offer up Jesus for us?

In chapter 3, looking at the role of the Holy Spirit in our salvation, I wrote that real love doesn't have to be earned. If it depended on the other person's agreement, it wouldn't be love at all, it would be a contract. So real love means you have to behave lovingly toward people even when they behave nastily to you. That means being vulnerable and willing to suffer. The Holy Spirit gives us the ultimate example of that kind of sacrificial love by coming into us sinners who hate him so much, giving new birth to hearts that would never choose it, and continuing to dwell in us as we constantly grieve him and defile his temple (ourselves) with our sins. What must it be like for him to be so intimately bonded with us and to love us so much while having a perfect divine knowledge of, and a perfect divine revulsion at, the heinousness of our sins— hour by hour, day after day, year upon year?

Now we come to something different. In the last three chapters, where I surveyed the work of God in our salvation, my main purpose was to show that only God does the work. We don't participate in the accomplishment of our salvation by getting plugged into a salvation system; Jesus accomplishes our salvation on the cross and in the empty tomb, because his saving love is personal. Our salvation is not determined by the workings of a system within nature; the Father alone determines it because saving us is his unconditional top priority. And the Holy Spirit does not give us a new birth because we consent to accept him; we come to accept him only because he has already given us the new birth—which he does because he loves us too much to abandon us merely on account of our rejection of him.

All those things are what God does. Now comes the part that we do. Calvinism does not say, as many people seem to think, that we have nothing to do in our salvation. It does say there are some parts of our salvation, like justification and regeneration, where we have nothing to do because God does it all. But there are other parts of our salvation where we have plenty to do. Sanctification, the process of becoming holy, is very much a part of our salvation, and it is very much something that we do (in cooperation with God, of course) rather than something God does entirely for us.

And the single most important thing that we do, the central thing that gives meaning to all the rest, is to accept and endure suffering. Sanctification is, in essence, learning to persevere in godliness through trials. The rest is details.

Sanctification means becoming holy. "You shall not profane my holy name, that I may be sanctified among the people of Israel. I am the LORD who sanctifies you" (Lev. 22:32). Becoming holy means becoming like God. "Consecrate yourselves therefore, and be holy, for I am holy" (Lev. 11:44). Becoming like God means, above all, loving—loving the way God loves: "Love your enemies and pray for those who persecute you, so that you may be sons of your Father who is in heaven. For he makes his sun rise on the evil and on the good, and sends rain on the just and on the unjust" (Matt. 5:44–45).

And what does loving the way God loves look like? The cross. That's what the Christian life looks like.

Suffering Is the Only Gateway to Joy

"The cross is a picture of the Christian life"—I'll bet that's not the message you expected when you picked up a book about "the joy of Calvinism"! Yet a willingness to persevere through suffering is the only gateway to joy. People who are determined never to suffer can never have joy because they can never love like God.

C. S. Lewis captured this point brilliantly in his incomparable masterpiece, *The Four Loves*:

> There is no safe investment. To love at all is to be vulnerable. Love anything, and your heart will certainly be wrung and possibly be broken. If you want to make sure of keeping it intact, you must give your heart to no one, not even to an animal. Wrap it carefully round with hobbies and little luxuries; avoid all entanglements; lock it up safe in the casket or coffin of your selfishness. But in that casket— safe, dark, motionless, airless—it will change. It will not be broken; it will become unbreakable, impenetrable, irredeemable. The alternative to tragedy, or at least to the risk of tragedy, is damnation. The only place outside Heaven where you can be perfectly safe from all the dangers and perturbations of love is Hell.[1]

It's only after you accept suffering that you can really have joy.

This is why times of suffering are often also times of joy. In fact, the most intense and unspeakable suffering can be an occasion for the most intense and unspeakable joy.

We usually think and talk as though this isn't true, as though it couldn't possibly be true. We assume that if we're feeling pain or grief or anger, we can't also be feeling joy. We think that if we were having an experience of joy at those times, that would somehow mean we were in denial about our pain, grief, anger, etc.—or, worse, not even having those feelings at all. It would be wrong and shameful not to feel grief at the death of a loved one, so we talk as though the grief were the only thing we could feel.

But it isn't so. I've experienced it myself a thousand times. My wife's chronic illness puts us—each of us separately, and both of us together—through more than enough trials. Many of them are very deathlike. The big deaths, like walking away from my last chance at an academic career, are actually not nearly as bad as the constant series of little deaths that we have to die our way through every day—the events we can't attend, the hobbies and activities we can't do, the struggle just to find time and energy for ordinary conversation and togetherness. My daughter's developmental challenges are another constant source of deaths; her period of war against God was infinitely worse for us because we were unable to communicate effectively with her about God. There are also the more common deaths that most Christians experience in one form or another, like having one of my dearest friends anathematize me because I wouldn't deny what I believed. And of course there are all the deaths, great and small, that are common to ordinary human life. Each of these has been an occasion of joy, joy right through the suffering—joy so intense that it would seem ludicrous if I tried to describe it in words.

I'm willing to bet you've experienced this, too. And you can see it operating constantly in all human culture. How many books, songs, movies, and shows are attractive to us because they convey the most extreme heights of anguish and joy at the same time?

The explanation is simple. We "rejoice in our sufferings" (Rom. 5:3) because we rejoice that our love perseveres. We know that suffering is always the real test of love—because real love is a way of behaving, is about setting priorities, and doesn't have to be earned. Whenever our love perseveres, we have the highest and best reason to rejoice. That's the reason Paul's much-quoted ode to love concludes with the triumphant—even defiant—proclamation "love never ends" (1 Cor. 13:8).

Love never ends! Most suffering is temporary in this life, and all suffering is brought to an end by death. Joy is not; joy never ends, because love never ends. While my love is persevering through a trial, I have both suffering and joy. But as soon as the trial is over, the suffering goes away. The joy remains. I carry forward with me the memory of the perseverance, the relationships that it strengthened, and the impact it had on my own character—all of which I can cherish and rejoice in for the rest of my life. And the joy remains even beyond that; it remains *beyond* the rest of my life. It remains forever. Not just a generic, diffuse feeling of joyfulness but the particular, very specific joy of having persevered through that particular, very specific trial. I can celebrate that joy for eternity. Love never ends.

From this we can learn a crucial lesson about joy. We tend to talk about joy as though it were a warm, fuzzy feeling of happiness, or (even worse) a form of pleasure. People are often deeply, profoundly challenged in their faith because the Bible tells them that relying on God always produces joy no matter what the circumstance (1 Thess. 5:16–18), and they think they don't have joy because they don't have feelings of happiness. There's no end to the spiritual dysfunction this can cause.

Well, I didn't have warm, fuzzy feelings of happiness when I was walking around with a bowling ball in my stomach because my daughter wouldn't stop cursing God. But even then, along with the anguish, I sometimes experienced what can only be described as joy. Later, especially in the next chapter, I'll come back to this mysterious experience we call "joy" at greater length. For now, I just want to stress that joy is not always fun. Our emotional and spiritual states are much more complicated than we usually assume.

Nothing can give us joy except love—because God is love, and we're made in God's image. And the only test of love is suffering. So joy and suffering are inextricably linked. No one knows this better than Jesus, who had to go to the cross before he could climb out of the tomb. Likewise for us; the suffering of the cross is a picture of the Christian life, but so is the joy of the empty tomb.

Each one actually derives all its meaning from the other. The cross wouldn't have saved us if Christ hadn't triumphantly risen again; without the resurrection, the crucifixion is worthless. That is the main point of Paul's famous treatise on the resurrection: "If Christ has not been raised, then our preaching is in vain and your faith is in vain" (1 Cor. 15:14). But on the other hand, the treatise begins by grounding its whole account of the resurrection in the work of the cross: "Christ died for our sins" (1 Cor. 15:3). Just as the cross wouldn't save us if it didn't culminate in the resurrection, the resurrection wouldn't save us if it weren't the culmination of the cross.

So while the bad news is that the only way to have the joy of the empty tomb in our own lives is to take up our crosses and suffer, the good news is that taking up our crosses does always—always—lead to joy in the end. They're two sides of the same coin; if you have one, you will have the other. You may have to wait a long time to get to joy, but get there you will, and usually sooner than you expect. All the unspeakable, overwhelming joy of that proclamation, "Christ is risen!" can come over us and pour through every fiber of our being at any moment in the Christian life. We have joy not in spite of our endurance of suffering but precisely because of it. We experience empty-tomb joy—not as an alternative to, but along with and as part of the bearing of our crosses and the dying every day. He who seeks to save his life will lose it, but he who gives up his life will find it.

It Hurts to Love God

The principle that real love means acceptance of suffering applies to all our human loves. But it applies all the more to our love for God. It takes a lot more suffering and self-renunciation for fallen and sinful creatures like us to love a holy God than it does for us to love each other.

It shouldn't be so, because God is the perfect object of love. For good measure, to help encourage our love for God, we can also remember that God loves us perfectly and always will. Yet precisely because God is the perfect object of love and loves us perfectly, he wants us to have joy—and since he knows that only love can bring joy, he cannot rest satisfied with anything less than perfect love in us. Our fellow creatures are satisfied with much less, but God knows we can't be really blessed unless we love him perfectly. And while our fellow creatures only see our outward behavior, God knows our minds, hearts, and spirits, and he insists on perfect love in all of them. Of course, none of us sinners actually loves with the perfect love that God knows is the only satisfactory love for us.

So since he loves us perfectly—ruthlessly, relentlessly—he's determined to grow that perfect love within us at any cost, even the cost of the cross.

That's why the Bible insists that suffering is essential to loving God. When James wrote about the difference between a living faith that changes the heart and a dead "faith" that is superficial and empty, he emphasized that the key difference is perseverance through suffering: "Count it all joy, my brothers, when you meet trials of various kinds, for you know that the testing of your faith produces steadfastness. And let steadfastness have its full effect, that you may be perfect and complete, lacking in nothing. . . . Blessed is the man who remains steadfast under trial, for when he has stood the test he will receive the crown of life, which God has promised to those who love him" (James 1:2–4, 12).

Calvin insisted on this point far more centrally than any Christian leader today that I know of. In our time, perseverance through suffering is a special topic that Christian leaders usually write and talk about separately. We have a special subgenre of books about the role of suffering. You can go to special conferences on it. Well, Calvin never wrote a special book about suffering or held a separate conference on it. *Having the joy of God by persevering through suffering was a central theme of all his writing about the Christian life.*[2]

Commenting on Philippians 4:4 ("Rejoice in the Lord always; again I will say, Rejoice"), Calvin comments that it is a particular mark of believers that they rejoice through suffering. He adds that times of suffering are when the joy of God has the most power in our lives:

> It is an exhortation suited to the times; for, as the condition of believers was exceedingly troubled and dangers threatened them on every side, it was possible that they might give way, overcome by grief or impatience. Hence he instructs them that, amid circumstances of hostility and disturbance, they should nevertheless rejoice in the Lord; as assuredly these spiritual consolations, by means of which the Lord refreshes and gladdens us, ought most of all to show their effectiveness when the whole world tempts us to despair.[3]

Commenting on James 1:2, a passage I quoted from just above, Calvin remarks that all forms of suffering and adversity are tests—and they always produce one of two outcomes. Suffering always ends in either failure or joy:

> That we may know more fully what he means, we must doubtless understand "temptations" or "trials" as including all adversities; they are called this because they are the tests of our obedience to God. He bids the faithful, while suffering these, to rejoice. . . . When he bids us to count it all joy, it is the same as though he had said: Trials ought to be counted as gain and regarded as occasions of joy. He means, in short, that there is nothing in afflictions which ought to disturb our joy. And thus he not only commands us to bear adversities calmly, and with an even mind, but shows us that this is a reason why the faithful should rejoice when pressed down by them.
>
> It is, indeed, certain that all the senses of our nature are formed in such a way that every trial produces grief and sorrow in us. . . . But this does not prevent the children of God from rising, by the guidance of the Spirit, above the sorrow of the flesh. That is why in trouble they do not cease to rejoice.[4]

Calvin was a man who knew what it's like to suffer for God. He suffered constant persecution for his gospel witness, from living on the run as a young man with a death mark in France, to coming out of his house one day in Geneva to discover an angry mob waiting to threaten his life. He passed up the opportunity to marry nobility in order to marry a sickly widow with two children. They had one child—who died shortly after birth.

In addition to the trials of his wife's health, his own health was regularly afflicted. Consider this passage from a letter to another reformer:

> At present, I am relieved from very acute suffering, having been delivered of a calculus [i.e. kidney stone] about the size of the kernel of a filbert [i.e. hazelnut]. As the retention of the urine is very painful to me, by the advice of my physician, I got upon horseback that the jolting might assist me in discharging the calculus. On my return home I was surprised to find that I emitted discolored blood instead of urine. The following day the calculus had forced its way from the

bladder into the urethra. Hence still more excruciating tortures. For more than half an hour I endeavored to disengage myself from it by a violent agitation of my whole body. I gained nothing by that, but obtained a slight relief by fomentations with warm water. Meanwhile, the urinary canal was so much lacerated that copious discharges of blood flowed from it. It seems to me now that I begin to live anew for the last two days since I am delivered from these pains.[5]

Immediately following this, he calmly returns to discussing the business of the Reformation. I am convinced that Calvin became a great theologian and reformer primarily because he learned how to suffer for God.

The Miraculous Gift of Perseverance

We must firmly grasp the deep interconnectedness of joy and suffering in order to understand the Calvinist doctrine traditionally known as "the perseverance of the saints." People who are truly converted to God will never fully and finally turn back because God creates in them, by the miraculous power of the Holy Spirit, a love for him that is so powerful it perseveres through all trials. If we are true Christians, our love for God is unbreakable because God's love for us is unbreakable, and his wonder-working power is always at work in us.

For the natural man, trials produce resentment toward God. For the new man, trials produce the joy of God because our love perseveres through suffering. The spirit of sin still has a presence in us, of course, but we now have a much more powerful Spirit planted in us by God's love. No trial can ever break our love for God because the more trials we endure the more we get the joy of God.

And we know that our new selves, the ones that respond to trials with joy, will always endure because we were re-created by God for precisely that purpose. Peter expresses the core doctrine of the perseverance of the saints when he writes that God "has caused us to be born again to a living hope . . . to an inheritance that is imperishable, undefiled, and unfading, kept in heaven for you, who by

God's power are being guarded through faith for a salvation ready to be revealed in the last time" (1 Pet. 1:3–5). He immediately adds that this salvation expresses itself in our lives as a faith that produces joy because it endures through trials: "In this you rejoice, though now for a little while, if necessary, you have been grieved by various trials, so that the tested genuineness of your faith—more precious than gold that perishes though it is tested by fire—may be found to result in praise and glory and honor at the revelation of Jesus Christ" (1 Pet. 1:6–7). Our faith glorifies God because its perseverance manifests its "tested genuineness" and thus inspires "praise and glory and honor" for Christ.

Don't get me wrong; the suffering itself is still suffering. I'm not trying to deny that pain is painful. Pain hurts. But the knowledge that God ordained my suffering in advance, from all eternity, in order to infallibly use it for my good radically transforms my attitude toward pain. An old joke runs: What did the Calvinist say after he fell down the stairs? "Glad I got that over with."

And I don't want anyone to get the idea that a true believer never fails in the face of a trial! Of course we fail. Although we're saved, we're still sinners. The very essence of sin is the failure to perform as God expects during a trial. So, being sinners, naturally we fail all the time—every day, in fact.

The point is that our love for God perseveres even through the trial of our own failure and sin. Our failure to do the right thing during a trial is itself another trial. In Psalm 51, David doesn't just lament his guilt and ask forgiveness but powerfully expresses how sin and repentance are a burden he must learn to carry for the Lord. He particularly asks for a restoration of joy: "Let me hear joy and gladness; let the bones that you have broken rejoice. . . . Restore to me the joy of your salvation, and uphold me with a willing spirit" (Ps. 51:8, 12). Even through the trial of failure, the trial of inadequate faith, our faith endures. The perfect Spirit of God within us always keeps flooding his perfect love into us, creating in us a love of God that is not yet perfect (because we're still sinners) but that endures even through the trial of its own imperfection and ultimately finds joy in that endurance.

Compare the two men who betrayed Jesus on the day of his death. After betraying the Lord, Judas gave up and killed himself. Peter went out from the disciples and wept bitterly, but he never stopped loving the Lord. Jesus knew that full well; that's why he restored Peter to the disciples by asking three times: "Do you love me?" (John 21:15–19). That's why he had his angel send specifically for Peter, by name, to reclaim him (Mark 16:7). And that's why Peter, after he had persevered through the trial of his own failure, had the joy of God in the end.

The Lord always summons us and reclaims us when we fail. Because he loves us personally and saves us personally, he sends for us personally—by name—as he did for Peter. And, like Peter, we always end with joy.

Sanctification Is Joy through Suffering

Lately many Calvinists have stopped using the phrase "perseverance of the saints." They're concerned that this phrase implies we persevere by our own strength, not by the strength of the Holy Spirit. Alternatives like "preservation of the saints" have emerged, emphasizing that the strength by which we endure comes from God.

It's certainly true that our perseverance is God's work in us, and it's important to keep that clear. But I'm gravely concerned about this new development for three reasons. First, alternative labels like "preservation" may create the impression that because God does the preserving, we do nothing. In fact, we cooperate with God in this aspect of our salvation.[6] Second, these alternative labels don't have the same clear connection to the process of sanctification. People are naturally concerned that telling people they can't lose their salvation may seem to deemphasize the call to holiness, and phrases like "preservation of the saints" fail to make the necessity of holiness clear. Third and by far the most important, these alternative phrases completely omit the central role of suffering in our endurance. And when you omit the suffering, you omit the joy.

The doctrine of the perseverance of the saints does imply that a saved person cannot lose his salvation—"once saved, always saved" as the trite and oversimplified phrase puts it. But the doctrine cannot be reduced to just that. Much, much more is being asserted here. The doctrine is that God makes us holy by first creating in our hearts a love for him that responds to trials with joy, then sending trials to test and purify us—consuming our dross and refining our gold (Prov. 17:3; Isa. 1:25)—knowing that the trials can never break our love for him, because our love for him is also from him.

Some people talk about sanctification as though it were all joy. Others talk about it as though it were all suffering. Both approaches are inadequate. If it were all joy and no suffering, there would be no progress in holiness; sinners like us can't get holy without a lot of dying to self. And if it were all suffering and no joy, it would be legalistic and self-righteous; we'd be getting "holy" like the Pharisees, pursuing the law through bare moral rectitude, cleaning the cup on the outside, forgetting that the highest law is love.

Sanctification is joy through suffering. Nothing else will do. It's a virtuous circle: we willingly accept suffering because we love God and have the joy of God; through suffering we prove our love and renew our joy; the proven love and renewed joy equip us to accept more suffering, producing more joy, and so on and so on— until we die or the Lord returns in glory. That's the program.

And God can put us through this process "safely," so to speak, because no trial can ever break our love for him. That love is there by his miraculous power, sustained by the presence and work of his Spirit in our hearts. God is holding both ends of the rope—he is at work both in the trial we encounter, which comes from God through his providential control of events, and in the love within us that endures the trial, which comes from God through the Holy

Spirit. All things, inside us as well as outside, work together for the good of those who love him.

Every Step Fits Together

As I've already pointed out, the observations I've been making about love follow from one another in a logical sequence. Real love is personal; therefore real love is a behavior, not a feeling; therefore real love is about setting priorities, real love doesn't have to be earned, and the only real test of love is a willingness to endure suffering.

The doctrine of the perseverance of the saints follows logically from the other doctrines I've outlined in the same way. God's saving love is personal; therefore Jesus completely accomplishes our salvation; therefore the Father chose us unconditionally, and the Holy Spirit miraculously transforms us; therefore our love for God will persevere through all trials.[7]

If Jesus actually accomplished my salvation, it follows that I will in fact be saved. All events in my own spiritual journey— turbulent though they may be—are simply the outworking of the salvation that has already been accomplished and planted within me. If it were possible for anything to prevent my salvation from growing all the way to full fruition, then that salvation was not actually accomplished by Jesus before it was planted in me.

If the Father chose me unconditionally, it follows that I will in fact be saved. My salvation is more important to the Father than anything in the system of nature, so nothing in the system of nature—including my own nature, my thoughts, feelings, desires, and decisions—can stand against my salvation. If it were possible for anything in the universe to prevent my salvation, then there must be something in the universe (such as the system of human nature) that God values more than my salvation. Otherwise, why would he allow the thing that blocked my salvation—whatever it is—to exist in the first place?

If the Holy Spirit converts me miraculously by a wholly supernatural act, it follows that I will in fact be saved. The Spirit did not have to struggle against my sinful resistance and win me over before he could give me the new birth. He just miraculously transcended my sinfulness and changed my nature. If he can do that, obviously no sin I commit can expel him or undo his work in me. The Holy Spirit is God, and my sins can't expel him from my heart any more than they can expel the Father from his heavenly throne; my sins can't undo his work in my heart any more than they can undo Jesus's work on the cross. If I were capable of undoing the Spirit's work, then that work was always dependent upon my natural cooperation or acquiescence, and therefore it was never a wholly supernatural transformation to begin with.

In the last chapter, I insisted on an unpleasant fact about us fallen people. Without the work of the Holy Spirit, we will never, never, ever fully and truly choose God. We may feel like we want to do it, we may regret our failure to do it, and we may even sometimes deceive ourselves into thinking that we've done it. But we will never finally give up that last tenacious grasp on self-will and put ourselves in his hands. We will always freely choose not to.

That fact has a flip side. Those who have been regenerated by the Holy Spirit will never, never, ever fully and truly give up on God. We may sin heinously, as Peter did when he betrayed the Lord. But we will never finally give up on God, as Judas did when *he* betrayed the Lord. We will always go on loving God. And God will always go on sending his angel to call us back—by name.

The perseverance of the saints is sometimes called the only point of Calvinism that people actually like. We recoil from the idea that Jesus doesn't do his saving work to save everyone. We recoil from the idea that the Father doesn't value everyone's salvation equally. We recoil from the idea that the natural man will always use his free will to freely reject God, and that the Holy Spirit therefore must change us by supernatural power rather than by persuasion. But we do like the idea that we don't have to worry about losing our salvation—that we are safe in God's hands.

Well, there is certainly an unspeakable comfort and reassurance in that. But I hope at this point I've shown that there's also great comfort and reassurance in those other doctrines as well. That's because they are, in the end, the same doctrine. And I've also tried to show that there's much to recoil from in the doctrine of our perseverance. The doctrine is not that you get saved and then all is well and it's happy, happy fun time for the rest of your life. The doctrine is that because God's love is unbreakable, God can hold you fast to himself while using trials and suffering and death to self every day to make you into the perfect child he created you to be.

If God Doesn't Do It, We're on Our Own
Other theological traditions agree that perseverance in faith is the key to salvation. That's not surprising; they read it in Scripture just like we do. Those who persevere in faith to the end will be saved. Those who turn away will be lost.

But while other traditions believe perseverance in faith is the key to salvation, most of them do not believe we are promised that perseverance. In fact, they specifically affirm that God does not provide perseverance; our perseverance is up to us. This, also, is not surprising; just as the Calvinist doctrine of perseverance follows necessarily from the other fundamental tenets of Calvinism, so the opposite doctrine follows necessarily from the rejection of those tenets.

If perseverance is not promised by God and provided by the work of the Spirit, it can only come from one place: my own strength, apart from God's work in my heart. The Calvinist does say that I persevere with "my" strength, but it's a strength that I have because God miraculously gives it to me. That's why I can be sure I will always have it. Those who deny the promise of perseverance must say that I persevere in "my" strength in a very different sense. God might help me in various ways, but in the end I must persevere with a strength that God does not give me.

This conclusion really cannot be avoided. The power of the Spirit in my heart will only operate to draw me toward God, never away. Therefore, if I turn away, it will be because my own natural will—whatever part of my will that was not transformed by God—decided to turn. So whether I persevere or fall away ultimately depends on the part of me that God does not transform. If the outcome of my spiritual journey is uncertain, the uncertainty can only depend on me; to whatever extent the outcome depends on God, it is not uncertain. My natural mind, heart, and will may be restored and aided by the work of the Spirit; but if that restoration and assistance actually removed the ultimate task of persevering from my natural will, it would thereby secure the absolute certainty of my perseverance.

The conclusion cannot be avoided because it is inherent in the premises. These traditions deny that God alone does the work of choosing us for salvation, accomplishing our salvation, and planting salvation within us. They attribute some role in these processes to human and other natural activity. So they can't avoid saying that whether they are saved in the end depends on whether they fulfill their roles. And whether they fulfill their roles is in their hands, not God's.

The Roman and Arminian traditions run parallel in this respect. They differ in critical ways about how people acquire faith. They therefore also differ about how people who have lost their faith can reacquire it. But about the loss of faith itself—the failure of perseverance—they agree. God provides help, and then (by definition) the rest is up to me to do with my natural strength. And the final outcome is determined by the part that's left up to my natural strength.

Lutheranism is the exception. Lutheran theology, as we have seen, denies the Calvinistic premises—the only premises that can possibly justify a promise of perseverance. But then Lutheranism seems to promise perseverance anyway.[8] Not being a professionally trained theological scholar, much less a scholar of the notoriously puzzling paradoxes of Lutheran theology, I feel comfortable admitting my ignorance as to how they can simultaneously hold these irreconcilable commitments. So I will remark no further on the matter.

Fear Is the Joy Killer

If we believe that we are not promised perseverance, the imperative to persevere takes on a radically different significance. If my fate ultimately depends on my own strength, I can never have confidence in my salvation.

If Christianity teaches anything, it teaches that only God is ultimately reliable. Other things are reliable only to the extent that God makes them so. The physical operations of matter, such as gravity, are reliable only because God causes them. "All things were created through him and for him. And he is before all things, and in him all things hold together" (Col. 1:16–17). The laws of logic are reliable only because they reflect the operations of God's mind, for "he cannot deny himself" (2 Tim. 2:13). Even Jesus went out of his way to insist that he was a perfect man only because he was God. "Why do you call me good? No one is good except God alone" (Luke 18:19).

If Jesus is perfect only because of his unique status as the man who is God, where does that leave the rest of us? If our perseverance ultimately relies on ourselves without God's guarantee, placing any kind of secure confidence in it would contradict all the fabric of Christianity.

Lack of assurance about salvation—which, alas, is a widespread problem among all theological traditions—is the most common reason believers don't have more and deeper experiences of joy. They know their salvation depends on their perseverance in faith, and they know that they are unreliable sinners. So they naturally tend to assume their perseverance is in doubt.[9]

Nothing kills joy like fear. I've already written that joy can coexist with many other emotions, like grief, pain, or anger. But it doesn't coexist with fear. This is all over the Bible. Consider what Paul writes:

Rejoice in the Lord always; again I will say, Rejoice. Let your reasonableness be known to everyone. The Lord is at hand; do not be anxious about anything, but in everything by prayer and supplication with thanksgiving let your requests be made known to God. And the peace of God, which surpasses all understanding, will guard your hearts and your minds in Christ Jesus. (Phil. 4:4–7)

The opposite of joy is not pain, or grief, or sorrow. It's fear. Do not be anxious about anything, Paul writes, and the peace of God will guard your hearts and minds. The absence of anxiety and the presence of spiritual peace—in other words, the certainty of our salvation—is what guards our hearts and minds.

Or, put more simply, perfect love casts out fear. John explains why: "There is no fear in love, but perfect love casts out fear. For fear has to do with punishment, and whoever fears has not been perfected in love" (1 John 4:18). Only Calvinism fully sustains the doctrine of the Christian life that's encapsulated in that sentence, because only Calvinism assures us that we will never see punishment because we will persevere in faith.

More specifically, believers who reject the Calvinistic doctrine must confront suffering without the promise of perseverance. For them, suffering is a completely different experience. The Calvinist can say, "God will get me through this." Others must say, "Will I get through this with God?"

What Does Suffering Remind You Of?
But there is also another challenge, arising not from the experience of suffering in itself, but from what the suffering points to. To the Calvinist, suffering is a constant reminder that God is still cleansing him of sin. To others, however, suffering is a constant reminder that God cares about other things more than he cares about our salvation.

No one can fully explain the phenomenon of suffering. That's because suffering is a result of the fall, the fall resulted from sin, and no one can fully explain the phenomenon of sin. Hence Paul writes of "the mystery of lawlessness" (2 Thess. 2:7).

But in a more limited way, the Calvinist can explain suffering as one of the ways God simultaneously works outside us and inside us to cleanse us of our sinful self-will. The reminder is partly unpleasant, because it reminds us that we're still sinful. But it is also partly reassuring, because it reminds us that God is working all things (outside us and inside us) together for our good. This explanation is satisfactory only because the Calvinist knows the sanctification process is, so to speak, "safe." God is at work in our hearts to ensure the ultimate outcome.

Other theological traditions cannot rest with this explanation. They can begin with it: God sends trials to refine our faith. But then they must answer the question: Why does God do this when he knows that some people—and for all I know I may yet turn out to be one of them—will fall away and be lost forever as a result? In their view, some suffering sanctifies but other suffering causes eternal damnation. Why does that second kind of suffering occur?

We saw in chapter 2 that if God doesn't unconditionally choose us for salvation, it follows that God is leaving our salvation in the hands of the general system of nature. From this, it further follows that God values the system of nature more than any particular person's salvation. Suffering must be accounted for within this framework.

Hence the non-Calvinist ultimately must say that we suffer because God values nature more than us. No doubt much of our suffering has the effect of sanctifying us, and since God is ultimately in control of the universe we can say that he uses some suffering for the purpose of sanctification. But that is really secondary. The primary explanation for suffering is that nature is God's top priority and we come second.

In one sense, this makes suffering easier to explain. When unbelievers challenge us to say how we can believe in a loving God when there's so much suffering, we can simply reply, "God does love us, but he loves nature more. We are the collateral damage in the great cosmic love affair between God and nature."

Yet this explanation succeeds by effacing the character of Christian piety. Gone is the God who smashes through all obstacles to save us. Gone—explained away—is the doctrine that God works all things together for the good of those who love him. In short, gone is the God who loves us above all else.

No One Sees Personal Love in Michael Novak's God

Consider the case of Michael Novak's *No One Sees God*. A response to the recent raft of militant atheist tracts, it is a brilliant book, in equal parts spiritual and sociopolitical. Yet when Novak answers the atheists on why there is so much meaningless suffering in the world, he offers an answer that is as simple as it is chilling. Novak, writing from within the Roman tradition, cannot say that the apparently meaningless suffering is not really meaningless, because God is secretly working all events together for our benefit. The suffering that appears meaningless must really be meaningless. Meaningless suffering, then, must be something God values and created for a good reason:

> Many rationalists argue that this God must be a bumbler. They can imagine a far more perfect world. More perfect in what respect? We have seen that Jefferson holds in the *Virginia Statute for Religious Liberty* that the Almighty might have made the world without human liberty. But, for reasons that escape us, He did not. For reasons not known to us, He made a world of probabilities, chance, hazard, contradictory tendencies, competitions, struggle, pain as well as pleasure, many stories of frustration and failure, as well as some with happy endings. Such a metaphysical vision of the real world that God did create seems remarkably compatible with the world of evolutionary chance and competition and odd harmonies described by Darwin and other empirical discoverers. . . .
>
> Clearly, He could have created a simple paradise of goodness, mutual cooperation, and trust, and peace on earth. The story of Adam and Eve in paradise holds before our eyes just this possibility. Instead, it seems, God allowed the human story to be one of weakness, betrayal, and evil by the free choice of many, and severe trial for the good who are also tempted by evil (seeing all its rewards on this earth).
>
> God as He reveals himself to Jews and Christians has somehow

imagined this earth as a great stage, an immense drama, a drama of liberty, and of the misuse and noble use of power, and of love and also betrayal. It is a play worthy of an Aeschylus, a Dante, a Shakespeare, a Milton, a Goethe. It is not a prettified morality play. It is ironic and tragic—and yet, withal, a comedy.

Heather [MacDonald] notes that the father driving the car that hit a train in Los Angeles read a sign wrong and paid for it with his life. Would she really prefer that all of us were robots who could never err on our own, never fail, never come to grief? When the Creator in fact chose to bring out of nothingness the contingencies and happenstances of this world as we see them, in its absurdities and tragedies, and if He took pleasure in the whole ("He saw it, and it was good"), then He had to allow a great deal of rope to human liberty. An open world order hospitable to freedom requires a world of wild contingencies, some ironic and some tragic.[10]

Here we have the whole non-Calvinist Christian world picture, presented in miniature. What God values, intends, and causes by his all-powerful will to be is not the particular outcome of this or that person, such as that father and child who were hit by a train. It is the whole gigantic mass of good and bad all jumbled together— what Novak calls "the whole." That's what God wants. If you happen to be one of the unfortunate victims who get pulverized because they were unlucky enough to end up in one of the bad parts of "the whole," you can take comfort in knowing that although God could have spared you, he let you get pulverized because the jumbled-up, partially meaningless "whole" is what God wants, and he couldn't have that "whole" unless at least a few suckers like you took it on the chin. (Note that Novak has contempt for the idea of a world in which we "could never err on our own, never fail, never come to grief." What does he think heaven will be like?)

Novak himself admits forthrightly that this approach, while it provides a simple explanation for suffering, gives us a God who is and must always be, to all appearances, cruel and insufferable:

The Jewish and Christian God makes no secret of being a God who in the full view of humans acts in a manner that is cruel, unfair, and terribly tormenting. Consider Job, his seven sons and three daughters killed, his property seized and livestock dead, his body covered with painful sores, pitiful.

The Christian revelation borrows heavily from this vision. Just look at what happens to Jesus, God's own Son, in his passion and death. If this is what God does to his Son, Scripture seems to suggest, we should not expect better treatment for ourselves. We are told, in fact, to pick up our cross and get ready to bear trial and suffering, as Christ did. As Job before him did.

Moreover, there is parable after parable about how unjust God is: He warmly embraces His prodigal son while turning his back on His dutiful, hardworking, self-denying brother; He pays workers in the vineyard the same wage even though some have worked all day and others only an hour; and there are many other such parables. God is just? Not by human standards. Not in the Christian Testament.[11]

By contrast, the God of Calvinism—who loves us personally and unconditionally—makes all things work together for our good.

However, Calvinism requires us to confront a more deeply perplexing mystery. If God can transcend our will to give us the new birth without suffering (as the Calvinistic doctrine implies), why does he then use suffering for our sanctification? We know that for sinners, to love a holy God requires much death to self, and hence suffering. But God transcends that limitation when he gives us the new birth. Why not transcend it all the time, or else transcend it all at once and make us perfect right at the beginning?

We don't know. That is a frustrating ignorance. But we do know that this is the way God has chosen to work, and we know that it must be good—and not just good but for our good, because all things work together for our good.

The Calvinistic approach calls upon us to trust God more radically. That is the deepest reason the Calvinistic approach leads to assured hope and greater joy.

Conclusion

The Joy of Calvinism

"Joy is not an emotion."

The pastor began his sermon with those words. It was a very large church, and the service was packed; I believe it was either Easter or Christmas, though I can't remember which. What I do remember clearly is what the pastor said next, because it was one of the most powerful moments I've ever experienced in worship.

I remember not only the words but the tone and cadence with which he spoke them. This particular pastor—Jim Engle—had a great gift for preaching. One aspect of his gift was his ability to be simultaneously emphatic and gentle. He could speak a scriptural truth not only with certainty but with what I would call a directed certainty—not the calm, inwardly focused certainty of the mystic (he didn't have a mystical bone in his body), but a dynamic certainty with an outward-driving force, as though he were pushing the truth toward you. Yet his tone was so mild and irenic that while his words carried force, there was no hint of forcefulness. He was the very opposite of aggressive. He was just a warm and kind man who very much wanted you to be aware of what God's Word said.

For a man with that gift, it's not surprising he ran our evangelism training ministry. I had gotten to know him well from attending the weekly classes, and treasured the gift of his teaching. But I was unprepared for what he had to say that morning.

Speaking slowly and calmly, but with great power, he began: "Joy is not an emotion. Joy is a settled certainty that God is in control."

I don't remember the rest of the sermon. I do remember, though, that it ended with exactly the same words that began it: "Joy is not an emotion. Joy is a settled certainty that God is in control."

My walk with God has never been the same.

Switch Off the Soap Opera

We think too much about ourselves. We aren't just selfish, we're self-centered. We don't just grab all the swag we can get our hands on, whether it's money, praise, advantages in relationships, cheap thrills, or just slothful inertia. We think constantly about how much swag we've got or haven't got.

And the worst form of our self-centeredness is probably our petty, fussy, and narcissistic obsession with our own mental states. For some, that includes an obsession with our own opinions—carefully keeping track of what we think about everything. For others, it includes an obsession with the decisions we make. For example, some people are indecisive or fickle because that lets them wallow in the pleasure of being in control. While you're in the process of making a decision you're in a position of power, but that power is gone as soon as the decision is made.

But almost all of us pay too much attention to our own emotions. We're happy, we're despondent, we're in love, we're lonely, we're thrilled, we're bored—we're a bunch of drama queens. We're each the star of our very own prime-time soap opera. True, my show's audience is small, consisting only of God and myself. And the critics hate it—God is always giving my soap opera negative reviews, urging me to switch the channel and watch something else for a change. But in spite of all that, I just can't help thinking everyone around me would really love my show if only I could get any of them to quit watching their shows (which are boring anyway) and watch mine instead. Besides, who cares what anyone else thinks—when I can simultaneously write, direct, and star in the *My Feelings Show*, why watch anything else?

This attitude not only arises from our sinfulness, it perpetuates it. This is one of the ways we keep our neighbors' needs well out of our own consciousness so we don't have to think about them. Instead, we can think about how our neighbors' actions are making us feel—reducing the people around us to tools we can use for our own self-dramatizing. And of course an obsession with one's own emotions is a wonderful way to anesthetize ourselves to the awareness of God. I find the biggest obstacle to prayer, for example, is that I keep turning my attention away from God so I can think about my own emotions while I pray. Am I reverent? Am I sincere? Am I sensing the presence of God?

This brings us right back to where we started, all the way back at the beginning. Love is not an emotion; it's a way of behaving. We like to wallow in the emotion of love so we don't have to pay the price of actually behaving lovingly. The more we deal with our neighbors by having feelings about them, the less we sense any need to do something for them.

To really love, we have to switch off the soap opera of the self and shoulder the burden of loving our neighbor in deed and not in cheap talk. And if we do that, we will suffer. Merely to switch off the soap opera involves a certain amount of death to self. To switch it off and then prioritize other people's needs above my own desires involves much more. As we have seen in the last chapter, it is the essential nature of love to be willing to suffer.

But suffering sanctifies us. It teaches us to see our own weakness and sinfulness. Above all, it teaches us to rely on God's strength rather than our own. And the more we rely on God's strength, the more we abandon the pretense that we are the captains of our souls, the more we realize that we could never do anything really worth doing on our own, the more we acknowledge that everything we have and are is the result of God's work—the more we do all this, the more we become aware that God is controlling the outcome.

That awareness is joy. We don't get joy by seeking a better emotional life, because joy is not an emotion. It is a settled certainty

Conclusion

that God is in control. And we get it by sacrificially loving God and our neighbor.

Imagine a Universe Where God Is in Control

I have tried to show that Calvinism, if consistently applied throughout heart, mind, and action, produces radically different results in the life of the believer. But that isn't because Calvinism itself is radically different from other theological traditions. In fact, Calvinism starts in the same place all the other traditions start. The difference is that Calvinism stays there.

All Christianity begins with the helplessness of sinful man and the power of God to save. We settled that issue back in the fifth and sixth centuries, in the struggle against the various legalistic heresies arising from the teachings of Pelagius. The orthodox church drew a line in the sand, declaring that true Christianity rests on the belief that the power of salvation lies with God. Augustine, who laid out the comprehensive orthodox case against Pelagius, referred salvation back to the sovereign and unconditional choice of God to save, and to save some people in particular but not others. All the existing branches of historic Christianity trace their lineage back through the orthodox church that rejected Pelagius and the all the various "semi-Pelagians" who arose after him. That is why all branches of Christianity are permeated by confessions, rituals, and behaviors that all presuppose our total dependence on God for salvation. In all Christian traditions, everywhere you turn you find people talking and acting as though everything depended on God and nothing depended on ourselves.

And yet, before the Pelagian conflict was even settled, the orthodox church was already compromising. While there have always been some who upheld Augustine's anti-Pelagian understanding of grace in all its fullness, most of the church pulled back. A comfortable halfway-house position was approved, whereby the sinner was said to have no effective power to contribute to his salvation, but could decide whether to accept or reject God's efficacious power.

148

Conclusion

The theological traditions other than Calvinism are, in various ways, the heirs of this compromise position. Thus, alongside all the various confessions, rituals, and behaviors that presuppose our total dependence on God, everywhere you turn you will also find other confessions, rituals, and behaviors that presuppose the reverse.

Meanwhile, Calvinism is the heir of the uncompromised Augustinian position. The development of doctrine in the tradition that traces its history back through Calvin has really been just the long, slow historical process of working out all the implications of the Augustinian understanding of grace.

The great question, of course, is which position is right. We might stop to quibble over words and phrases, asking how it is possible to say the sinner's salvation depends on his decision to accept God, yet that decision exercises no "effective power" of salvation. If his decision is what determines the outcome, it is "effective" in the only sense that really counts. And if his decision is the only thing that determines the outcome, then his decision is really the only thing that is "effective."

Yet the deeper issue here is not the question of efficacy. It is the question of control. The compromise position, in its various expressions, puts us in control of our salvation—to the exclusion of God's control. The Calvinist position keeps God in control of all things at all levels. Calvinism affirms that we have free will; we are indeed in control of our own actions. But our control of our actions does not exclude God's control of all events, including our own actions. And it is God who determines the outcome of my salvation.

As B. B. Warfield put it, only the Calvinist "sees God behind all phenomena, and in all that occurs recognizes the hand of God, working out his will."[1] Nothing occurs in God's universe except what he has willed to use for his own good ends, preeminently the manifestation of his love for his people. That gives us a radically different universe.

The compromise conceptions invite us to imagine a universe divided into two sections. In one section, God's will reigns supreme. In the other section, God has chosen to give up control. He calls upon us to do what he tells us is right, but he is not guiding the outcome. The stakes are as high as they possibly can be—our eternal bliss or misery—and God has left us to succeed or fail by our own strength.

The picture is, as we have seen, self-contradictory and impossible in many respects. Jesus's death on the cross is substitutionary, but impersonal. God knows everything, but undertakes "conditional" or "hypothetical" actions. God wants everyone to be saved, but delegates their actual salvation to the unfolding of the system of nature. The Holy Spirit draws us to God, yet we decide for ourselves whether to come to him. And so forth. To cite Warfield again, "We fancy that God controls the universe just enough to control it, and that he does not control it just enough not to control it."[2]

Yet suppose it were not self-contradictory. Would it be consistent with God's character as we come to know him in the Bible? What kind of God would abandon us to such a universe?

The Calvinistic conception, by contrast, invites us to imagine a universe in which God is in control. This is certainly very disturbing when we contemplate the occurrence of sin, suffering, and damnation in a universe that is totally under God's control. Yet, as I have tried to show throughout this book, the realities of sin, suffering, and damnation are even more disturbing when we contemplate them occurring in a universe that is *not* totally under God's control. Only God's control can imbue these disturbing realities with a redeeming structure of meaning. We are not adrift in a chaotic universe where God allows things to happen that don't serve a good purpose. It is only because God is just and holy—with all the horrifying implications that fact carries for guilty sinners like us—that we can safely love him and trust him. The Calvinistic picture has not only the merit of being internally consistent and the merit of being consistent with God's character as revealed in the Bible. It is also, in the end, the only picture of the universe in which there is any secure comfort.

Joy is a settled certainty that God is in control.

Freedom from Fear

People talk about the "five points of Calvinism." J. I. Packer once wrote that there are not truly five points of Calvinism but only one. The one point of Calvinism is that God saves sinners.[3]

Calvinism makes me fully aware of my release from the bondage to the law. As long as I think that I'm in control of my salvation, I can never fully escape from fear. I don't mean the reverential "fear" of God as a majestic father, which is good and pure in believers. I'm talking about the slavish fear of God's wrath against sin—precisely what the bondage of the law produces. Of course, believers who think they control their salvation are not actually in bondage to the law; if they were, they wouldn't be believers. But they will always feel and act to some extent as though they were still in bondage.

As long as I retain a false consciousness of bondage to the law, my obedience to God can never be fully selfless. I will struggle to remain faithful at least partly out of a slavish fear of wrath rather than the godly fear of reverence. I struggle because my immortal soul depends on it. And to obey out of that kind of fear is not really to obey at all. It is self-serving. I'm still serving myself. I'm still starring in my own soap opera.

Calvinism, by contrast, assures me that I am God's child forever, that all things work together for my good, and that in the end I will stand before the throne and be accepted. There is no need to struggle for my immortal soul; Jesus did all that on the cross. There is no more fear of wrath; Jesus took all that on the cross. There is nothing left but reverence and gratitude, and the joyful discipleship they produce.

True obedience to God emerges when reverential awe and joyful gratitude flow together in the absence of the slavish fear of wrath. The more control we attribute to God, the more we are purged of the slavish fear of wrath—perfect love casts out fear—and the more we will be filled with gratitude to him. The Calvinist, by attributing all control to God, can have an obedience that is unambiguously free from fear.

This is why, as we saw in the last chapter, fear is the opposite of joy, the joy-killer. Joy is a settled certainty that God is in control.

Unconditional Grace and the Fullness of Eternal Joy

Most highly of all, only Calvinism consistently teaches that nothing glorifies God more than his saving love for me. Calvinism actually unites two things that the other traditions, at best, merely hold together in a state of paradoxical tension: the glory of God's holiness and his love for a sinner like me.

We usually encounter God's holiness and his grace to us as sinners separately. We encounter them separately when we're first evangelized, in the message of the gospel: we're sinners destined for hell because God is holy, but salvation is available in Jesus because God loves us anyway. We continue to encounter them separately in worship when we are reminded that God is holy and we're sinners, and then reminded that God loves us anyway and saved us in Jesus. And we encounter them separately in our relations with the world, where we are sometimes called to affirm what's good (which is really affirming that God's sustaining grace is still at work in the fallen world) and sometimes called to oppose what's bad (which is really affirming that God is holy).

Perhaps it's inevitable that finite creatures like us, with our limited perspective, will constantly have to break down the reality of God's attributes into separate pieces in order to think about them. But we need to remember that God is not made up of parts. He's all one thing, simple and indivisible, and all his attributes are unified in his being.

Unfortunately, all other theological traditions besides Calvinism create an artificial difficulty in reconciling God's holiness with his grace to us. The separateness with which we encounter these two aspects of God hardens into a paradox. As a result, whatever we may think in our heads, in our hearts we never feel quite fully that we glorify God.

The problem begins right at the beginning, when these traditions differentiate (implicitly if not in so many words) between God's love for "humanity" in the abstract and his love for individual human beings. As we saw in chapter 2, they hold that for God the salvation of humanity in the abstract is more valuable than anything else, but not the salvation of any particular people. In other words, God desires above all that salvation should occur, but his desire that any particular person be saved is subordinate to other values. Of course, none of us individual people is actually saved in the abstract. So the love that actually saves us is, on this view, merely hypothetical or conditional. God will save us, but only on the condition that other things don't intervene.

God's holiness is absolute. But, in this view, the love that saves us is not absolute. It is conditional. And of course both of these facts must remain as they are forever. If God's saving love for me is conditional in eternity past, it isn't going to become unconditional in eternity future. There's only one eternity, and it doesn't change. So on this view we must imagine ourselves standing before God for eternity, knowing that he is absolutely holy but not absolutely grace-filled toward us.

With this picture, we can never really feel quite at home with the supreme love that saves us. We will always carry around the knowledge that in standing before a holy God, we are—and always will be—second rate. We were saved, not because God loved us so much that he reordered everything in the whole universe for the sake of our salvation, but because he was able (fortunately!) to squeeze us into his agenda, to fit in our salvation along with the other more important things he had going on in the universe. We are not the crowning glory of God, but merely one of the gems in the cosmic crown of nature—and a gem that, in God's view, didn't really need to be there.

The Calvinist view, having declined to compromise the personal quality of God's love at the beginning, provides a radically different picture here at the end. For the Calvinist, God's love for us is as absolute as his holiness. Just as God's saving work reaches all the way down to the bottom of the unfathomable depths of our sin, his saving love goes all the way up to the very core of the divine Being. His holiness does not require him to demote us in the great scheme of his valuations. In all the universe, we are his very favorite, the created beings that glorify him most.

The Westminster Catechism, the standard Calvinist catechism in the English-speaking world, begins by asking what the chief purpose of man is. The answer: "To glorify God and enjoy him forever." C. S. Lewis, citing this answer, commented that they are really the same thing in the end. We glorify God by enjoying him, and enjoy him by glorifying him. "Fully to enjoy is to glorify. In commanding us to glorify him, God is inviting us to enjoy him."[4]

It was a deeply wise observation. Indeed, he was wiser than he knew, for he never understood the full meaning. In heaven we will have the full joy of God for the same reason we will fully glorify him—because we will fully know that he is in control, and always was, and always will be. Only through that truth can we truly place all our trust, all our hope, and all our love in God without reservation; and only through that truth can we receive back the full joy of God.

Appendix

Questions and Answers

1) So who was this John Calvin guy, anyway?
2) What about the "five points of Calvinism" or TULIP?
3) What about "four-point Calvinism"?
4) Wait a minute. Didn't Calvin himself endorse "four-point Calvinism" at one point?
5) What about free will? How can we have free will if God ordains everything?
6) Doesn't Calvinism say we are naturally "unable" to stop sinning? How are we truly guilty of sin if we're not able to stop?
7) If God ordains everything that happens, doesn't that imply God caused the fall?
8) Doesn't the Bible say God wants everyone to be saved?
9) Doesn't the Bible say God doesn't "show partiality"?
10) Doesn't Calvinism undermine evangelism?
11) Doesn't Calvinism say you can be absolutely sure you're saved? Isn't that arrogant?
12) What about the passage where it says. . . ?

This book is not a traditional apologetic for Calvinism. A traditional apologetic would have been constantly turning aside from the main narrative to address more technical questions arising from specific scriptural, philosophical, or historical concerns. I have not done that. My reason is simple: all those questions have already been addressed by others, and far better than I could do myself. I saw no point in reinventing the wheel. Indeed, the traditional apologetics for Calvinism have been dealing with the more scholarly and technical issues so well that I'm afraid we may be losing sight of what ought to be the main narrative—hence I saw a need for a book that set down the main narrative without turning aside to technicalities at all.

But of course it is very unlikely that anyone will pick up this book never having encountered Calvinism in any way before. And if you've encountered Calvinism (either directly from Calvinists or indirectly from what other people say about it), you probably have questions about it that can only be answered by pursuing some of those more technical issues that I have excluded from this book.

If you are seeking a traditional apologetic for Calvinism, you have many fine books from which to select. In the last generation, the classic popular work has been R. C. Sproul's *Chosen by God*. Perhaps I'm old fashioned—okay, I'm definitely old fashioned—but I still think that is the best place to start. More recent books have included James Boice and Philip Ryken's *The Doctrines of Grace*, Michael Horton's *Putting Amazing Back into Grace* and *Introducing Covenant Theology*, R. C. Sproul's *What Is Reformed Theology?* (previously published as *Grace Unknown*), and Robert Peterson and Michael Williams's *Why I Am Not an Arminian*. A less traditional approach is taken in Richard Mouw's *Calvinism in the Las Vegas Airport*. (My apologies to anyone whose book I've neglected; there are too many for me to provide a complete list.)

On another note, I have been tremendously helped by the recent *John Calvin: A Heart for Devotion, Doctrine, and Doxology*, edited by Burk Parsons. I think readers who are new to Calvin and Calvinism will be, too. The book includes some apologetic for Calvinism but is much more focused on providing a well-rounded overview of the man John Calvin and the content of his writing and ministry.

Nonetheless, it will probably be of use if I provide you with short summary statements of the Calvinistic view on some of these more technical questions, as well as brief answers to some other questions typically asked about Calvinism. Let me caution you that these are only intended to be brief summaries to tell you what the Calvinistic view is, rather than a fully developed case supporting that view. If you want to hear the fully developed case for the defense, you can easily find that elsewhere, and from people who have scholarly knowledge that I don't possess. What I hope to do here is draw you a road map to the issues in order to clear up any initial misunderstandings you may have and help you figure out which questions you really need to know more about. Once you know that, you will be better able to figure out where to go next for further study.

1) So who was this John Calvin guy, anyway?

Have you heard the old saying that if you want to make God laugh, tell him your plans? Calvin's whole life was like that.

Jean Calvin—known to us as "John" Calvin—was born in France, sixty miles north of Paris, in 1509. Like almost everyone in France, he was raised in the Roman church. There was a growing evangelical movement in France; the great gospel revival known as the Reformation had been sweeping through Germany since 1517 and was spilling over the border. But the French Reformation was all underground at that time because the king, Francis I, had suppressed it.

Calvin's father first set him on course to study for the priesthood, then switched him over to law—the two fields in which the young Martin Luther was also trained. Ironically, it was during his legal studies and not his studies for the priesthood that Calvin, one of the most important Bible scholars in history, learned Greek.

After his father's death, Calvin studied more broadly. The new "humanist" academic movement was emphasizing the study of classic works and fields of inquiry that had been neglected in the Middle Ages, and this new direction of scholarship was key to producing the intellectual leadership of the Reformation—it was humanist research into the literature of late Roman antiquity that made the original works of Augustine available to Luther, with explosive results. But rather than take the knowledge produced by humanist scholars and become a church leader, as Luther had, Calvin felt called to the life of scholarship itself. Setting himself on a path to spend his life in the academy as a humanist scholar, he wrote his first book—what we would call his doctoral dissertation—on the ancient Roman legal and political philosopher Seneca.

At some point during this period of his life—we don't know the year—Calvin experienced an extremely powerful religious conversion. He described it thus:

> Since I was too obstinately devoted to the superstitions of popery to be easily extricated from so profound an abyss of mire, God by a sudden conversion subdued and brought my mind to a teachable frame, which was more hardened in such matters than might have been expected from one at my early period of life. Having thus received some taste and knowledge of true godliness I was immediately inflamed with so intense a desire to make progress therein, that although I did not altogether leave off other studies, I yet pursued them with less ardor.[1]

Overwhelmed by his experience of God's grace, he gradually migrated to the study of theology. And while he would go on to make contributions in many areas of this discipline, his first love was always biblical exposition. He would rapidly become one of the greatest biblical expositors of all time, producing volume after volume of scholarly exegesis of Scripture.

In 1534, Francis began a crackdown on the underground evangelical movement in France, following an incident known as "the affair of the placards." In the dead of night, placards with evangelical slogans were hung throughout the city; one was even hung on the king's bedroom door. Calvin may have been implicated in the affair. It would not have been the first time the authorities had come after him for his evangelical sympathies; on one previous occasion he had escaped capture by tying sheets together and climbing down out of a bedroom window, then posing as a vine-dresser. After the affair of the placards, he decided to leave central France entirely and head for the German border. Since the study of the pure biblical gospel was banned in France, settling in Germany made more sense anyway if he wanted to pursue a life of theological scholarship.

While much of Germany was also closed to the gospel, there were a number of cities where it was welcomed. In a few of them, evangelical scholars were setting up shop and founding theological schools. Luther's Wittenberg was far away in the easternmost reaches of Germany, but one of the other leading German reformers, Martin Bucer, had set up a sort of western outpost of Lutheran scholarship in Strasbourg, right on the French border. Nearby towns, including Basel, were also welcoming evangelical scholars.

Calvin spent fourteen months in Basel and proved to be a prolific scholar. Among other writings, he produced the first edition of his great masterpiece, *The Institutes of the Christian Religion*. Rather than a systematic theology—Calvin never wrote a word of systematic theology in his whole life—it provided primarily two things: encouragement and pastoral guidance in the Christian life for French evangelicals who had no pastors to nurture them; and an apologetic answering the accusations brought against evangelicals by Francis and the Roman church. Both these intellectual projects were formed by Calvin's deep and wide-ranging Bible scholarship. The original 1536 edition was a mere 516 pages—a tiny trifle of a book compared to the length of the later editions Calvin would go on to produce, culminating in a final version of over 1,500 pages—but it was still a revolutionary work that electrified the French-speaking world with the gospel of free grace in Christ. The evangelical movement in France would expand like wildfire under its influence.

Later that year, there was a temporary amnesty for evangelicals and Calvin made a brief return to Paris. But he didn't stay long. He had made up his mind to settle in Strasbourg and give himself over wholly to serving God's emerging evangelical movement through theological scholarship.

However, this plan—like the priesthood, like the law, like humanist scholarship—was not God's plan for Calvin. Francis and

Charles V, the German emperor, were in the middle of one of their endless wars. (Charles had just been awarded the German emperorship and Francis had been his main rival for that position, so the two of them were not friendly neighbors.) The most recent locus of fighting lay directly between Paris and Strasbourg. To reach his intended destination safely, he would have to detour far to the south, through western Switzerland.

Calvin made a stop in Geneva, which had emerged as a significant battleground in the expansion of the Reformation. Zurich, in eastern Switzerland, had been one of the earliest and strongest centers of the Reformation. In Geneva, by contrast, the gospel had gone in and out of favor and was constantly hanging by a thread.

The root of the conflict was a division between the population at large and the wealthy elites. The people wanted the city to have a Reformation church. The elites didn't object to that in principle, but they insisted that the church had to maintain the extremely loose moral standards that had prevailed before the Reformation. Under the Roman church, they had grown accustomed to having their cake and eating it too—openly and shamelessly indulging in adultery and other heinous sins, while also enjoying the respectability of church membership. (The word "libertine" in its modern meaning was originally used to describe the Genevan elites during this period.) But the people demanded Reformation pastors, and Reformation pastors demanded the right to administer a basic level of church discipline—denying membership and the sacraments to people living openly anti-Christian lives.[2] Since Geneva had a mixed constitution that allowed some power to both groups, neither group could get its way entirely, and the city was constantly swerving and lurching in one direction and then the other.

For ten years prior to Calvin's arrival, the hot-tempered Guillaume Farel had led the city's Reformation movement. Farel quickly realized that Calvin, who outwardly seemed to be a quiet scholar, had the potential to become the titanic reformational leader that he had been praying God would send to Geneva.

Calvin's talents went far beyond his prolific writing abilities. He could preach, he could teach, he could pray, he could organize, he could lead, he could counsel the perplexed, he could comfort the distressed, he could discipline the recalcitrant, and (perhaps most important in Geneva) he could stand fast in the faith under persecution.

Farel insisted that Calvin should stay in Geneva, because God had brought him there to bring the city fully into the Reformation. At first, Calvin refused. Although he was bold (often too bold, to the point of nastiness) in defending what he believed, he was personally a modest man and did not see himself as a ministry leader, still less a great reformer. But Farel insisted. As Calvin made preparations to leave for Strasbourg, Farel's temper got the better of him. He angrily denounced Calvin to his face for turning away from the calling of God. After anguished prayer, Calvin reconsidered and decided to stay.

But he was not to stay long—God had yet another change of plans in store. Almost immediately, Calvin came into conflict with the city elders over control of church discipline. Calvin insisted that church discipline belonged to the church, not to the civil authorities (as was the case in Zurich). Matters came to a head when Calvin refused to give the sacrament of the Lord's Supper to a wealthy citizen whose life was openly immoral. The city council ordered Calvin to deliver the sacrament, and he refused.

For defiance of the city's authority, Calvin was banished in 1538. He took up his former plan to settle in Strasbourg and spent the next three years there, expanding the *Institutes* and producing a French translation of the Psalms, among much else.

He also felt the need to marry. He turned down an offer of marriage to a woman of noble birth, commenting to a friend that he wouldn't marry that woman "unless the Lord had entirely bereft me of my wits." He instead chose Idelette de Bure, a woman in his congregation with two children, whose husband had died in a plague. They were married in 1540 and were greatly happy, but not for long. Their only child, Jacques, would die shortly after birth in 1542. Calvin wrote to a friend, Pierre Viret, that his only consolation was in God's control of all events: God "is himself a Father, and knows what is best for his children."[3] Idelette, who had always suffered from chronic illness, died in 1549. Describing his extreme grief to Viret, he wrote that God's supernatural control of his heart was the only reason he did not break down entirely: "You know well enough how tender, or rather soft, my mind is. Had not a powerful self-control, therefore, been vouchsafed to me, I could not have born up so long."[4]

As Calvin was settling in for a life of scholarship in Strasbourg, God changed his plans again. The political winds shifted in Geneva and the city invited him back. At first he declined the offer, but in 1541 he decided to return. On the first Sunday after his arrival, when he mounted the pulpit to deliver the sermon, he surprised his congregants by saying nothing about his exile and return. Instead, he picked up and continued his preaching series exactly where he had left off three years earlier.

From 1541 until his death in 1564, Calvin worked tirelessly to advance the cause of the gospel. He became a far greater reformer than he or even Farel had dreamed possible. His spiritual and intellectual leadership not only established the Reformation in Geneva but exported it around the world.

Under Calvin's leadership, Geneva eventually became a model for how the gospel could radically transform a community. Calvin focused on teaching people to live the gospel with their whole lives, to see their daily activities in the home and in their occupations as the front lines in the spiritual war with Satan. Church and religious works became helps and supports, not the central focus. At last, the people of Geneva were guided in how to live the gospel lives that they had been hungering after for decades. And the elites, no longer able to have their cake and eat it too, were more or less brought into line with the needs of public morals.

He didn't do everything right, of course. Probably most important, Calvin rejected freedom of religion—an idea espoused, though not fully practiced, by Luther—as unbiblical. In this, he followed what was the overwhelming majority view of the times. However, that is not a very good excuse for a man whose whole life had been dedicated to challenging "the overwhelming majority view of the times" from a biblical standpoint. The passage in the *Institutes* arguing against freedom of religion is embarrassing to read.

But it would be wrong to make too much out of this issue. There were very few cases of actual persecution; we only know of a handful. The spiritual transformation of Geneva was not accomplished by force; it was accomplished by some of the best preaching and teaching any ministry leader ever provided. Freedom of religion was just not a highly important issue in a small, theologically homogeneous community like Geneva. There weren't many religious dissenters running around in this agricultural community way up in the Swiss mountains. It was in places like London and Paris where they fought over freedom of religion. The big fights in Geneva were centered on issues like civil vs. church control of church discipline. In fact, by asserting the right of the church to control its own discipline (unlike the way things had gone in Zurich) and by developing a relatively democratic church governance structure (unlike the way things had gone in Germany), Calvin laid critical groundwork for the later emergence of religious freedom.

And Calvin turned Geneva, a multilingual city, into a staging ground for the spread of the gospel in France, and then England, Scotland, the Netherlands, and eventually (through them) the New World. First, a flood of French-language books and treatises began flowing over the border into France—especially the *Institutes*, which was to sixteenth-century France what *Mere Christianity* was to twentieth-century England. Then French evangelical scholars and ministry leaders began coming to Geneva to study and equip themselves. Then, during a period of intense persecution in England and Scotland, a whole generation of English-speaking evangelical scholars and ministry leaders settled in Geneva. They produced their own flood of Bible translations, books, and so forth—including the world's first study Bible, known as the Geneva Bible, which provided a new English translation of the Scriptures, with notes in the margins to explain the meaning of difficult passages. When England and Scotland became open to the gospel again, their evangelical leaders returned from Geneva equipped and encouraged for radical gospel ministry.

Thus it was Calvin's work in Geneva that was primarily responsible for the spread of Protestantism to the larger world in the sixteenth century. Lutheranism never reached beyond the Germanic and Scandinavian countries, and its reach was imperfect even there. The Anabaptist traditions did not come into their own until later. In the evangelization of the globe that took place during the first century of the Reformation, Calvin is the pivotal figure.

2) What about the "five points of Calvinism" or TULIP?

In our time, most people talk about Calvinism in terms of something called "the five points of Calvinism." But the five points are not—and were never meant to be—either a full statement of Calvinistic doctrine, or a clear statement of Calvinistic doctrine, or a precise statement of Calvinistic doctrine. They are a mnemonic device; their purpose is to help you remember what Calvinism says—on the assumption that you have already learned and understood it from other, more fully and clearly articulated sources. So even if the five points were doing their intended job correctly, they still would not be a summary statement of the core identity of Calvinism. And in fact the five points don't even do their intended job correctly, because the understanding of Calvinism that they help people to remember isn't accurate.

The "five points" mnemonic device is an acrostic—five phrases forming the word TULIP:

T—total depravity
U—unconditional election
L—limited atonement
I—irresistible grace
P—perseverance of the saints

The image of a tulip was once a useful memory device for people who wanted to remember the content of Calvinism, because Calvinism used to be widely associated with the Netherlands. (Hard to believe that today, isn't it?)

There is a popular myth that these five points originated at the Synod of Dort in 1618–1619. This myth persists because Dort did produce a set of "canons" or primary findings, and the canons centered around five teachings that the synod labeled "main points of doctrine." Thus it is true that there was, at Dort, a set of five points. They're just a different set of points from the five points of the TULIP acronym. TULIP was an effort to summarize the five points of Dort, but it was a failed effort. There's not much that's actually shared between TULIP and Dort except the number five.[5]

The historical record is, here as in every other case, difficult to piece together. A certain level of uncertainty is unavoidable in any historical inquiry. What follows is the best summary of the evidence that seems to me to be possible.

TULIP originated in the twentieth century. It was not even widely used until the second half of the twentieth century. Some nineteenth-century writers referred to "five points of Calvinism," but they were referring either to the Canons of Dort or to various other summaries of those canons, not to TULIP. The earliest known appearance of TULIP is a 1913 magazine article, which attributes the acronym to a lecture the author had attended in 1905. Even then, the acronym was fluid, and the exact phrasing of the TULIP points seems to have changed over time. (In the 1905 lecture the U stood for "universal sovereignty.") And, interestingly, the 1913 article compares TULIP to a variety of other formulations that purport to summarize "the five points"; the various formulations differ

dramatically from one another. Of the lot, TULIP is the least similar to the actual content of Dort. It appears that the final version of
TULIP was solidified by its appearance in Lorraine Boettner's 1932
The Reformed Doctrine of Predestination. Boettner appears to have
been the only important Calvinist writer to use TULIP at any time in
the first half of the twentieth century. However, the landmark 1963
book *The Five Points of Calvinism Defined, Defended and Documented*,
by David Steele and Curtis Thomas, erroneously equated TULIP
with the long-standing, traditional five points that had defined
Calvinism since Dort. After that, the myth that TULIP summarizes
the canons of Dort seems to have become widely accepted.[6]

The difference between TULIP and the original five points of
Dort matters for two reasons. First, the doctrinal formulas adopted
at the Synod of Dort are far superior to the formulations used in
TULIP. Falsely attributing TULIP to Dort causes us to overlook the
much better theological statements Dort provides. Second and
more important, attributing TULIP to Dort makes it appear to be
much more important to the history and identity of Calvinism
than it really is. It makes TULIP look like an early development
that grew out of Calvinism's formative years, when in fact it was
a late development that played no role in Calvinism's formation.
It makes TULIP look like it was carefully crafted by a large conven-
tion of top theologians, when in fact it seems to have been made
up by one person, passed around and changed for a while, and
then stumbled onto center stage by accident. And it makes TULIP
look like it was adopted during one of the most important defining moments in the history of Calvinism's development, when in
fact it was just somebody's attempt to provide people with an easy
mnemonic device.

TULIP is not without some merit. It does a good job of display-
ing the deeply Trinitarian character of Calvinistic doctrine:

State of man before salvation: total depravity
Work of the Father in salvation: unconditional election

Work of the Son in salvation: limited atonement
Work of the Spirit in salvation: irresistible grace
State of man after salvation: perseverance of the saints

TULIP highlights the organic unity of the work of the three persons in the Calvinist understanding.

Also, the function we now use it for—to draw boundaries around Calvinism, to say what Calvinism denies—is a legitimate and important function. A theology that cannot say what it denies cannot really say what it believes. We require denials as a bulwark against backsliding.

Nonetheless, I hope I have made it clear that I think the demerits of TULIP far outweigh its merits. To begin with, the technical and negative side of a theology is never the place to start learning about it, much less the place to start learning and then stop. You cannot find out what a theology teaches by learning only what it denies.

More important than that, though, the terminology used in TULIP actively invites misunderstanding. In at least one case, "total depravity," the term asserts what Calvinism in fact denies (as we saw in the Detour at the beginning of this book).

If we must express Calvinism in five abbreviated phrases corresponding to the pattern of the five points, we might do better with this:

State of man before salvation: wholly defiled
Work of the Father in salvation: unconditional choice
Work of the Son in salvation: personal salvation
Work of the Spirit in salvation: supernatural transformation
State of man after salvation: in faith, perseverance

This gives us the handy mnemonic WUPSI, pronounced "whoopsie"—as in, "Whoopsie, we just realized that TULIP is giving everyone heinously false ideas of what Calvinism is all about." Perhaps it's not as memorable as TULIP, but it has other virtues to make up for that.

3) What about "four-point Calvinism"?

As people have come to think about Calvinism almost exclusively in terms of the five points, one of the interesting consequences has been the emergence of the label "four-point Calvinism" to describe some people's theological position. Many people find themselves agreeing with the first two points of TULIP (the *T* and the *U*) and the last two points (the *I* and the *P*) but disagreeing with the *L*. That is, they agree with the whole Calvinistic system except for what it says about Christ's work at the cross and the empty tomb.

I have never really understood this position. The four-pointers want to integrate a universalistic understanding of Christ's work— in which Christ dies to make atonement for all people as though they were all going to be saved—with an understanding of the Father's work and of the Spirit's work and of human nature that are all solidly antiuniversalistic. The pieces just don't fit together.

In the thoroughly non-Calvinist view, God knows that not all will be saved, but he desires the salvation of all people equally, and therefore the Father, Son, and Spirit each do their saving work as though it were possible for all to be saved. That is not ultimately defensible, in my view, but at least it is coherent. When Christ dies, he is acting on a hypothesis he knows to be false, which is absurd, but at least we are given a reason why we should think he would do so. The imperatives of maintaining the system of nature—including human free will—allegedly demand it.

In the four-point view, however, God does not just foresee that not all will be saved, but he is the one who ordains that not all will be saved. He is in control of all things, and he knows it, and he acts accordingly—except in Christ's work, where he suddenly acts as though he had not ordained what he did in fact ordain, and is not in control of what he does in fact control. It is as though God temporarily forgot that he was God.

Most astonishingly to me, this sudden interruption of God's benevolent providential superintendence of all events happens for no apparent reason. Because the four-pointers uphold the other four points, they deny all the universalistic premises that make the universalistic understanding of Christ's work coherent. Here there is no claim that Christ must act on premises he knows to be false in order to maintain the integrity of nature; no insistence that free will is incompatible with God's control of events.

But leave all that aside. Any view that rejects the Calvinistic understanding of Christ's work empties the cross and the tomb of their real meaning. Rather than actually saving us, Christ merely makes salvation available. This is as true for the four-pointers as for anyone else. The question "Why did Christ have to die, if his death did not actually accomplish people's salvation?" is just as embarrassing for the four-pointer as for the thorough non-Calvinist. The difference is that the thoroughgoing non-Calvinist can give us an explanation for why we should reduce our estimation of the power of the cross. The four-point Calvinist cannot. (That is, not systematically—of course there may be reasons for the position that are grounded in textual interpretation, but that is a different matter.)

4) Wait a minute. Didn't Calvin himself endorse "four-point Calvinism" at one point?

I honestly don't much care. I don't mean to be rude about this. I know people who have spent considerable portions of their lives studying this question, and I'm sure it will irk them to hear me say that I don't really care a lot about the object of their study. I'm not saying it's not a question worth studying. But that doesn't mean it's as important to all of us as it is to the specialized scholars whose job is to study these things.

There is a dispute among the scholars over whether some of Calvin's remarks can be reasonably interpreted as having expressed the four-point Calvinism view. It's not as simple a question as it might sound, because this is not a subject Calvin incorporated into his major works. There is no chapter in the *Institutes of the Christian Religion* entitled "Why I Am a Four-Point Calvinist," nor is there a chapter entitled "Why I Am Not a Four-Point Calvinist." Calvin did not incorporate this issue into his thinking systematically, which makes it complicated to examine what his opinion was, assuming he did have one.

Because the scholars disagree, the only way for a layman like me to find out the truth would be to engage in a serious study, reading what the scholars on each side have to say and weighing which ones seem to have better evidence and arguments. And, frankly, I just don't think it would be worth the investment.

Everyone makes mistakes. Calvin made lots of them. Even if we put this particular issue aside, I could probably name fifty things off the top of my head that I think Calvin got wrong. If it could be proved that Calvin once endorsed four-point Calvinism—well, then, that would make it fifty-one. Or if it could be proved that he didn't—well, then, it would still be fifty. If the four-point view were systematically asserted in Calvin's major works, that would be another issue. Since it isn't, the question of whether he made this mistake on some less central occasion is—well, less central.

History (especially intellectual history) is an important and worthy field. I'm glad there are people who spend their time going through the historical record and tracing the development of ideas among people like Calvin. I'm also glad there are people who study diseases in hopes of finding new and better treatments; that doesn't mean I feel obligated to keep up to date on all the latest cancer research.

What the layman like me is vitally interested in, what we really need to study and know what we think about, is not the history of a doctrine but its truth or falsehood. Once I see that four-point Calvinism has to be false, how much can I really be expected to care whether Calvin once espoused it?

The faith tradition that traces its history through Calvin developed a coherent body of theology not long after Calvin himself left the scene. Calvin's disciples and followers spent the next few generations after his death building a systematic theology (Calvin himself never wrote systematic theology; in his writings he was a Bible expositor, pastor, and apologist). The coherent body of theology that emerged in the Calvinist tradition quickly came to adopt the view of Christ's work that I articulated in chapter 1. It did so for the obvious reason—because it is the only view of Christ's work that is consistent with the other fundamental premises of Calvinistic doctrine. As I said in the Detour at the beginning of this book, Calvinism presents an integrated Trinitarian theology in which the "high" view of the Father's work, the "high" view of the Son's work, and the "high" view of the Spirit's work are all mutually reinforcing. The principle underlying the whole system is that God uses his total control of all events to save his people—through his own work and to his own glory.

5) What about free will? How can we have free will if God ordains everything?

Calvinism says, just as strongly as any other tradition, that people have free will and are responsible for their actions. I've already mentioned (back in the Detour) that the phrase "free will" means different things to different people. Today, when we talk about "free will," we mean that people are responsible for their own choices; they're not just puppets of forces they can't control, such as heredity and environment. But the debate in the sixteenth century had nothing to do with that. When Erasmus, Luther, and Calvin talked about free will, they were debating whether people are born as slaves to sin, or are born free from slavery to sin—free to choose whether to become slaves of sin or slaves of Christ (1 Cor. 7:22). They all agreed that people are responsible for their own choices. Unfortunately, many people who have read deeply in the sixteenth-century debates use the term as it was used in those debates, not as it's typically used now.

But we have also seen that Calvinism says God is in control of everything—that he "ordains" everything that happens. To many people this seems like a flat contradiction. How can people have free will if God is in control?

All sensible Calvinists agree on the answer to that question. How can we have free will if God is in control? Beats us. We don't know. Color us stumped. All we know is that it happens; we do, in fact, have free will and God, in fact, is in control.

Just because we can't see how something can be true doesn't mean it isn't. I, for one, don't see how it could possibly be true that subatomic particles can physically exist but not be subject to what we normally call the "laws" of physics. Yet the entire profession of physicists—*almost* all of whom seem to be normal, sound-minded people and not psychotic pathological liars or delusional maniacs—says that some subatomic particles physically exist but do not occupy specific points in either space or time. They move from place to place without traversing the space in between. They even exert causal force on one another (i.e., a change in the motion of one directly and immediately causes a change in the motion of the other), even though they are separated in space and there appears to be nothing to transmit the causation from one to the other.

I cannot understand how that can be true. But I don't think God's freedom in making the universe is limited by my ability to understand his work. God can certainly make a universe in which subatomic particles behave in ways that I can't account for. The same applies to the freedom of the will and God's omnipotence.

We have to be careful about the difference between a real contradiction and a mystery or paradox. It's one thing to say that two things can't both be true. It's quite another thing to say that we can't understand how they both can be true.

If there is a real, flat, unavoidable contradiction between two statements—such as "$x = 1$" and "$x = 3$"—then they can't both be true. Logicians call this "the law of noncontradiction," and it is an absolute law. The reason is simple: God is one, and he will not both do something and not do it. "He cannot deny himself" (2 Tim. 2:13).

But sometimes two things appear, superficially, to be contradictory when in fact they're really not. That's how riddles and logic puzzles and magic tricks work. It's common in theology, too. Most people think "God is one being" and "God is three persons" is a flat, direct, unavoidable contradiction. They say these can't possibly both be true at the same time. They're wrong. It just looks like a contradiction to them because they stubbornly refuse to open their minds to how a transcendent creator God might not be what they expect him to be. They want a God who fits their preconceptions; they will not accept any other. And no wonder—if they admit that God might be something dramatically different from what they were expecting, they would really be admitting that they need to go find out what God is actually like rather than making up a tame "God" in their heads. And who knows where that might lead? The real God might not excuse my self-centeredness and my greed and envy and lust and sloth and hatred and resentment, the way the tame "God" I made up for myself does. It's much safer to just go on worshiping my made-up "God" and insist that anyone who challenges my preconceived notions about God is talking a bunch of self-contradictory nonsense.

The same principle applies to God's omnipotence and our free will. We must find out what the real universe is like, not cling to our preconceived notions. Once we admit that God is a transcendent, omnipotent creator beyond all possibility of full human comprehension, we have to give up our expectation that we will be able to understand everything about either him or our relations to him. We should expect to find many things that appear, at first, to be contradictory, but which turn out (once we study them) just to be mysterious paradoxes beyond our ability to grasp.

If God is omnipotent, he must order and direct all events. The key question is: once all of God's activity is accounted for, are there still multiple possibilities for how events might turn out within the created order? If so, God is not omnipotent, because there are things in creation that "go their own way" outside God's control. If not, then everything that happens is ordered and directed by God's activity.

I think most people insist so strongly that free will and God's control of events are contradictory because they are afraid that if they don't, they will end up having to deny that we have free will. If you feel that way, you can put those fears to rest. There is no possibility that any honest investigation of the question will ever lead us to deny our free will. The appearance to the contrary is mostly the result of confused language.

The Trinity demonstrates that the relationship between free will and control works differently when God is involved. Among us, two people can't have a real relationship if one of them is in complete and total control. Yet we know that within the Trinity a relationship of real love and real freedom—free will—exists between the three persons even though the Father is in complete and total control.

This may become more clear if we return to the Westminster Confession of Faith, which we looked at just a little bit in the Detour, and see what it says about free will and God's control of events. One section of the Confession, in the context of explaining the fall, asserts that God providentially controls all human actions without doing violence to human free will by "a most wise and powerful bounding, and otherwise ordering, and governing of them, in a manifold dispensation, to his own holy ends."[7] If God governed our actions by actually planting our decisions in us directly, our wills would not be free, and God would be the author of our sins. But he doesn't do that. He governs our actions indirectly, bounding and ordering them from the outside—that is, without directly authoring them.

All Christians believe that God does this sort of thing at least some of the time. There would be no other way to explain biblical events like the hardening of Pharaoh's heart. God pretty clearly exercises control over Pharaoh's decisions but without taking away Pharaoh's free will. We know Pharaoh still has free will because God blames Pharaoh for his actions. God's "hardening" of Pharaoh's heart therefore cannot mean that God reached inside (so to speak) Pharaoh's heart and planted hardness there; rather, he simply gave more freedom to the hardness that was already there. He didn't make Pharaoh evil; he just gave Pharaoh's evil a longer leash.

Calvinism just takes this same idea—that God can control events, even including human decisions, without violating our free will—and applies it to all human actions rather than just to some of them. So if the Calvinist view amounts to saying that God's providence negates free will, then all Christians say God's providence negates free will, and we're just quibbling over how often it does so. But I doubt many people will be comfortable framing the argument that way.

Or take what the Confession says about the work of the Spirit in converting a sinner to Christ. The Calvinist view of the Spirit's work is well summarized in the first section of the Confession's chapter on the subject:

> All those whom God hath predestinated unto life, and those only, he is pleased, in his appointed and accepted time, effectually to call, by his Word and Spirit, out of that state of sin and death, in which they are by nature, to grace and salvation, by Jesus Christ; enlightening their minds spiritually and savingly to understand the things of God, taking away their heart of stone, and giving unto them a heart of flesh; renewing their wills, and, by his almighty power, determining them to that which is good, and effectually drawing them to Jesus Christ: yet so, as they come most freely, being made willing by his grace. (WCF 10.1)

Obviously the most important part of this section for our purposes is the last part, which says that when the Spirit is "drawing them to Jesus Christ" they "come most freely." The Confession makes a point of insisting that the Spirit does not encounter resistance on our part and overcome it by force, or in any other way violate our free will.

But in addition to the explicit affirmation of free will, it's worth looking at the rest of the section to see how the Calvinistic understanding of the Spirit's work is consistent with our free will. The Confession says that in the new birth, the Spirit does the following:

- Enlightens our minds
- Removes our hearts of stone
- Gives us hearts of flesh
- Renews our wills
- Determines us to good
- Draws us to Jesus Christ

Is this description consistent with saying that we come to Jesus "freely" and "willing"?

Let's take these points one at a time. No one will dispute that you can enlighten someone's mind without violating his free will. Just for starters, if you thought otherwise you wouldn't be reading this book in the first place. It might enlighten your mind and thus destroy your free will!

The language about removing the heart of stone and implanting the heart of flesh is drawn directly from Scripture (Ezek. 11:19 and 36:26). Inner renewal is also a scriptural description of regeneration (Ps. 51:10; Rom. 12:2; 2 Cor. 4:16; Eph. 4:23; Col. 3:10 and Titus 3:5). So I expect nobody is going to quibble with those descriptions, either.

That leaves us with the phrase "by his almighty power, determining them to that which is good, and effectually drawing them to Jesus Christ." At first that may sound like it violates our free will. No doubt that's exactly why the authors of the Confession immediately rushed to add the words "yet so as they come most freely, being made willing by his grace"—they wanted to make it clear that they were *not* denying our free will.

The key issue here is that the Confession uses the word "determining" to describe the Spirit's effect on us. So we need to look at what the Confession means by this word. There are only two places where the Confession uses the word "determine," in some form, in connection with human will. The first is section 9.1, which—as we saw in the Detour—strongly affirms the freedom of the will by saying that "God hath endued the will of man with that natural liberty, that it is neither forced, nor, by any absolute necessity of nature, determined to good, or evil." The second place is the section we're now looking at, section 10.1, which also strongly affirms the freedom of the will.

Let's compare how the Confession uses "determine" in each case. Section 9.1 says the human will is not naturally "determined" by exterior forces like heredity and upbringing. Section 10.1 says the Spirit draws believers to Christ by supernaturally "determining" our wills to good.

The juxtaposition is startling and revealing. The authors of the Confession affirm the same thing in both cases: God is in control of events, but in a way that is consistent with human free will. However, it draws a distinction between God's supernatural "determining" of our hearts through the Spirit, and natural "determining" of the will by heredity and upbringing.

Natural "determining" would violate our free will. But God's supernatural "determining" transcends the limits of nature. By supernatural power, God is able to order and govern our hearts without interfering with the freedom of our wills. That's why the Confession denies that our decisions are "determined" by natural causes, but affirms that God "determines" events supernaturally. The former would negate our free will; the latter does not.

Unless you're prepared to say God violated Pharaoh's free will when he determined how Pharaoh would act—and then blamed Pharaoh for the very actions Pharaoh supposedly had no control over!—I don't see how you can avoid this conclusion. God is in control, yet we have free will. Nothing I can say will make the mystery any less mysterious. But there is no need, in Christianity, for us to pretend to understand mysteries. That's for Gnostics and Platonists. Merely coming to understand how mysterious the mystery is will give you all you really need to know about this subject.

6) Doesn't Calvinism say we are naturally "unable" to stop sinning? How are we truly guilty of sin if we're not able to stop?

Calvinism does say that the natural man, without the supernatural transformation of the Holy Spirit, is "unable" to turn to God, and even "unable" to do anything at all without sinning. This obviously prompts the objection: if we are really unable to stop sinning, how are we responsible for our sin?

To begin with, the language of inability is clearly warranted by Scripture. "Apart from me you can do nothing" (John 15:5). "Unless one is born again he cannot see the kingdom of God" (John 3:3). "A person cannot receive even one thing unless it is given him from heaven" (John 3:27). "When the disciples heard this, they were greatly astonished, saying, 'Who then can be saved?' But Jesus looked at them and said, 'With man this is impossible, but with God all things are possible'" (Matt. 19:25–26). When Calvinists say the natural man is unable to stop sinning and turn to God unless God changes him, they are only repeating what Scripture clearly teaches.

But what does it mean? We have to start by making a distinction between different senses of the word "inability." Calvinists distinguish between absolute inability and what they call "moral inability." This is something of a subtle point, but it is the only way to make sense of Scripture when it uses the language of inability to describe our natural state.

If you told me to lift a house off the ground, I might reply, "I could never do that!" And if you told me to murder my wife, I might likewise reply, "I could never do that!" But although I might use the same words, there is a critical difference in meaning. The word "could" means something different in the first sentence than it does in the second.

My inability to lift a house off the ground is an absolute inability. It's just a physical fact about the world, like the color of the sky or the coefficient of gravitation. However, my inability to murder my wife is very different. There is one sense in which I could, in fact, murder my wife. I have the physical ability to do it if I want to. But that's the catch—I can only do it if I want to. And in fact I would never want to. That is not an absolute inability, but it is still a real kind of inability.

It is a moral inability, because it arises from my character. There are some people in the world who really are morally able to kill their wives. They have a different character than I do. I'm not judging them spiritually—my inability to know their secret hearts is just about as absolute as an inability gets! For all I know, perhaps if I had been in their shoes I'd have turned out even worse than they did. But be that as it may, the plain fact is there for all to see: different people have different characters, and some people are morally unable to do things that others are morally able to do.

Shakespeare expresses this memorably in a scene (act 2, scene 2) from my favorite play, *Measure for Measure*. The self-righteous prig Lord Angelo has condemned a man to die for a relatively minor offense. The condemned man's sister, Isabella, comes to plead for her brother's life. The following exchange occurs:

> Isabella: Yes; I do think that you might pardon him,
>   And neither heaven nor man grieve at the mercy.
> Angelo: I will not do it.
> Isabella: But can you, if you would?
> Angelo: Look, what I will not, that I cannot do.

Lord Angelo summarizes in a nutshell the "inability" of fallen and sinful man to do good. "What I will not, that I cannot do." The natural man "cannot" stop sinning, not because he absolutely cannot stop, but because he will not stop. No matter what circumstances you put him in, no matter how much time you give him, he will never, never, ever stop. He will always freely choose to sin—because that's just the kind of people we are.

The same distinction can be seen in the way Scripture talks about God. Scripture sometimes says that God "can" break his Word, but won't (for example, Matt. 26:53–54) and sometimes says that God "cannot" break his Word (for example, 2 Tim. 2:13). The message is the same, but two different senses of "ability" are used to describe it.

And it should be obvious why this distinction matters so much. An absolute inability is something I'm not responsible for. Nobody blames me for my inability to lift a house off the ground. But a moral inability is something I'm responsible for. That is the very essence of the distinction. The whole difference between an absolute inability and a moral inability is precisely that a moral inability is my fault. Literally, it is "my fault"—a fault in me, in my character.

But this leads us on to an even deeper question. Calvinism says that all people have this flaw in their characters from the very beginning—from the womb. So how are we responsible for a character flaw that we're born with?

That is a very profound question, and I cannot pretend to do it justice here. I can only note that this question is not really a challenge to Calvinism. It's a challenge to Christianity. The doctrine of original sin stands or falls on this point, and the gospel stands or falls with the doctrine of original sin. The assertion that we cannot be responsible for a moral flaw if we're born with it is Pelagianism pure and simple. Once we have come to understand that the "inability" Calvinists talk about is a moral inability, there can really be no objection to it on grounds of our moral responsibility without cutting the legs out from under Christianity as a whole.

7) If God ordains everything that happens, doesn't that imply God caused the fall?

While many people have never thought about it, this issue has actually been one of the deepest sources of theological conflict over Calvinism. It is the essence of Calvinism to rejoice that God is in control of all phenomena. Why, then, the fall? Those who adhere to other traditions say the fall occurred because God gave humanity free will. For the Calvinist, this is insufficient; as we have seen, Calvinism says God is still in control even after he gives humanity free will. God could have made a world of creatures with free will who would not have fallen, but he chose not to. At least to some people, this seems to suggest that in some sense, on some level, God must have caused the fall.

First of all, the word "caused" is ambiguous. There are many different ways to cause something. Let's say the beloved mayor of a small town in Iowa dies, and the citizens vote in the town assembly to install a statue of him in the town square. The money is raised from local philanthropists. A sculptor acquires the marble and chisels the statue. A construction crew installs it in the town square. Now, who or what caused a statue of the dead mayor to be placed in the square? The citizens, the philanthropists, the sculptor, and the construction crew, obviously—though each in a different way. But what about the geologic forces that produced the marble? Or the American system of democratic government? Or the mayor himself, because he did things worth remembering? Or the cultural tradition by which beloved public figures are often honored after their deaths with statues? Or the artistic conventions of statuary? Or the people who settled the town a century earlier, without whom there would have been no town, and hence no town square, no mayor, and no statue? Or the railroad companies whose westward expansion made the town's settlement possible? Or the investors who loaned money to the railroad companies? Or Thomas Jefferson, who acquired Iowa in the Louisiana Purchase? Or George Washington, since there would have been no Louisiana Purchase without American independence? Or the colonists who settled America? Or . . .

All these things were as necessary to the statue's appearance in the town square as the citizens, the patrons, and the sculptor. Yet although they can all be called "causes" in one sense, not all these factors are responsible for the statue in the same way. The geologic forces that produced the marble, for example, are not *morally* responsible for the construction of the statue. Neither is George Washington.

Now let's return to our question. Calvinism certainly does imply that if God had wanted to, he could have made a world that didn't fall. But he chose to make a world that did. In that particular sense, you can say—if you insist—that God "caused" the fall.

I would definitely prefer to find some other way of talking about this whole issue without getting into the subject of who "caused" the fall. Our finite minds aren't really capable of understanding how causation works when we're dealing with the relations between an eternal God and the world he created. Once again, as with the question of free will, we are dealing with an issue beyond our comprehension. Or rather, we have just come around in a circle and are right back to dealing with that same issue. How does God's control of events relate to our free will? We don't know, and any pretense that we do is nonsense. We must take seriously our inability to understand such things.

But we have to talk about this issue somehow, so for the moment, let's stipulate that God "caused" the fall in the limited sense that he could have chosen to make a fall-proof world, but didn't. Even this would not make God responsible for the fall in the way that Adam and Eve were. The key difference is that God did not authorize the fall, just as geologic forces don't authorize the creation of statues.

Some people argue that we must say God didn't "cause" the fall in any sense, because otherwise he'd be responsible for the fall. But if we take that line, what are we to make of the promise that in heaven there is no sin and never will be for all eternity? How can God promise us that once we get to heaven we will be absolutely secure against sin forever?

Obviously if the Bible's promises about heaven are true, then God is able to make a world populated by beings with free will who never sin. He's made one in heaven. Once we admit that, there is no avoiding the implication (unless we're prepared to compromise God's omnipotence) that he could have made another such world on earth. But he didn't.

Moreover, all Christians agree that God was not compelled to create anything. This is a bedrock premise of all theology; without it we get modalistic pantheism, not a transcendent creator deity. God created "freely"—he created solely because he wished to. And when he created the world, he knew that it would fall.

Once we admit that much, we've admitted that God could have avoided the fall but chose not to. At this point the major issue has been conceded. No real argument remains other than quibbling over semantics.

So once again, the real objection here is not to Calvinism but to Christianity. Just as you can't object to the concept of moral inability without denying original sin, you can't object to God's choosing to permit the fall when he could have avoided it without denying either God's freedom or his foreknowledge. And both of those premises are necessary even to constitute serious theism, much less Christianity.

8) Doesn't the Bible say God wants everyone to be saved?

Calvinism says God could save everyone but chooses to save only some. However, there are some passages in the Bible that seem to say God wants everyone to be saved. "As I live, declares the Lord GOD, I have no pleasure in the death of the wicked, but that the wicked turn from his way and live; turn back, turn back from your evil ways, for why will you die, O house of Israel?" (Ezek. 33:11). I've already said a little about this subject in chapter 3, but it may help if I add a bit more development of the Calvinist position.

Some of the Bible passages people point to as establishing this are ambiguous. But whatever issues may arise in interpreting this or that particular passage, I think there is a pretty good case to be made that at least some passages do indicate that God wants everyone to be saved.

In one very important sense, Calvinism completely agrees that God does want everyone to be saved. The question is, in what sense? Absolutely? Or in a more limited way?

We saw above that the distinction between absolute "inability" and a more limited kind of "inability" is essential to making sense of Scripture. If we insisted that every time Scripture said we were "unable" to turn to God, it means absolutely unable, that would result in nonsense. The same is true here; we must be prepared to draw distinctions between absolute and limited senses of a word, or we will end up with nonsense.

Does God absolutely want everyone to be saved? If so, we will end up back on the merry-go-round that has been dogging us since chapter 1. If God absolutely wants everyone saved, then either everyone is saved (which we know is not true) or God fails to get what he wants (which we also know is not true).

In fact, God is not making absolute statements about his will, but telling us something very important about his character—if you like, about his attitude. God's attitude is such that he is open to reconciliation with any human being, without exception, who repents from sin. God's character is such that the whole human race could receive salvation, at any time, just by repenting. The only problem is that no one repents!

God tells us that he takes no pleasure in the death of the wicked because he wants to make it clear that we are the problem, not him. If these passages were not in Scripture, we might get the impression that God is resentful and hard hearted—that God hates our sin because he's arrogant and desires our worship and obedience to gratify his ego. By declaring that he is open to reconciliation with all who repent, God is making it clear that he is in no way arrogant or egotistical toward us. He hates our sin because it is sinful, not because he is in some way diminished by it.

One way Calvinists have talked about this is to say that there are two wills in God—or, to put it more precisely, there are two things in God that can both be called "God's will," but in two different senses of the term. There is what you might call his moral will, by which he ordains what people ought to do. And there is what you might call his providential will, by which he ordains what actually happens. (Theologians have a bewildering variety of technical terms for these concepts, but it isn't worth trying to keep track of them.) What God says we ought to do is "God's will" in one sense, and what God chooses to actually bring about is "God's will" in another sense. Regarding the salvation of all people, God morally wants all people to repent, but he does not providentially ordain that they all will.

Some people accuse Calvinists of believing in a "schizophrenic God" because they say there are two wills in God. But it seems to me that you must believe there are two different things that can both be called "God's will" whether you're a Calvinist or not. We all agree that God is good and omnipotent, yet evil occurs. Therefore, there are some things that are "God's will" in one sense yet not "God's will" in another sense.

And note that in general, God has the right to select which evils he will allow to occur and which he will prevent. Nobody says God is arbitrary or schizophrenic because he allows some evils to occur while intervening to prevent others. God can be equally opposed to all evil while allowing some evils to occur and not others. The same principle applies to the salvation of souls. God can have an attitude that is equally open to accepting repentance from all people yet intervene to bring some to repentance but not others.

9) Doesn't the Bible say God doesn't "show partiality"?

Calvinism says God doesn't value the salvation of all people equally. He chooses some people—his people—for whom he will intervene to ensure their salvation, because their salvation is the most important thing in the world to him. Others he passes over, allowing them to remain lost.

Yet one of the things the Bible insists on about God is that he is impartial. "God shows no partiality" (Acts 10:34; Rom. 2:11). How can we reconcile that with the idea that God values the salvation of some more than others?

When the Bible says God is impartial, clearly this cannot mean that he favors all people equally and never makes distinctions. We see God favoring some over others and making distinctions all the time. "The Lord had regard for Abel and his offering, but for Cain and his offering he had no regard" (Gen. 4:4–5). "Jacob I loved, but

Esau I hated" (Rom. 9:13). And among all Jesus's disciples, only one is called "the disciple whom he loved" (John 19:26).

If God had no favorites, the gospel would be nonsense. The gospel claims to tell us how we can have God's favor. The concept of "God's favor" would be meaningless if God had no favorites. And in fact the biblical authors are pretty clear that accepting the gospel means becoming one of God's favorites. "To all who did receive him, who believed in his name, he gave the right to become children of God" (John 1:12). "See what kind of love the Father has given to us, that we should be called children of God; and so we are" (1 John 3:1).

So it's not a question of whether God favors some over others. It's a question of why. Among human beings, when we say that someone acts "impartially," we don't mean that person never makes distinctions. We mean that person makes distinctions rightly or fairly. The "impartial" judge is not the judge who refuses to favor the innocent over the guilty. Quite the contrary! The impartial judge is precisely the judge who really does favor the innocent over the guilty—as opposed to, say, favoring the party who is socially higher, or who speaks more eloquently in court, or who shares the judge's political leanings, or could reward the judge financially. The impartial judge not only can "play favorites," but must do so—he must favor the right favorites, must favor the people he's supposed to favor. Otherwise he's not impartial at all.

Now apply this to God. When the Bible says that God is impartial, it doesn't mean he has no favorites. It means he favors people based on his good and holy judgment—he favors the people he ought to favor. God doesn't choose people based on their social status or any such nonsense. God is not a snob:

> For consider your calling, brothers: not many of you were wise according to worldly standards, not many were powerful, not many were of noble birth. But God chose what is foolish in the world to shame the wise; God chose what is weak in the world to shame the strong; God chose what is low and despised in the world, even things

that are not, to bring to nothing things that are, so that no human being might boast in the presence of God. And because of him you are in Christ Jesus, who became to us wisdom from God, righteousness and sanctification and redemption, so that, as it is written, "Let the one who boasts, boast in the Lord." (1 Cor. 1:26–31)

You can see this in the context of the passages that assert God's impartiality. In Acts 10 and Romans 2, national prejudices are in view. Peter discovers that the Lord has extended salvation to the Gentiles and exclaims: "Truly I understand that God shows no partiality, but in every nation anyone who fears him and does what is right is acceptable to him" (Acts 10:34–35). Paul explains to the believers in Rome that Jews and Greeks are subject to the same law and saved by the same gospel, "For God shows no partiality" (Rom. 2:11).

Of course, knowing that God doesn't favor people for the wrong reasons tells us nothing about which people God actually favors for the right reasons—the people he actually does, and rightly does, favor. The various theological traditions disagree about the basis for God's favoring some over others. Rome says he favors those who use the sacraments. Arminians say he favors those who believe the gospel. Calvinists say we don't know why he favors some over others, but we know that it isn't because of anything in them or anything they do. He must have a good reason in himself, one that glorifies himself, but we don't know what it is.

The point is that all of these views are equally compatible with saying God is "impartial." In all these views, God has favorites. In all these views, God favors those whom he ought to favor. Therefore, on all these views God is "impartial."

But if we really wanted to press the point and ask which tradition does the most justice to God's impartiality, it seems to me that there's a strong case to be made that it's Calvinism. After all, while all traditions agree that God doesn't favor people based on social status or eloquence or intelligence, the non-Calvinist traditions still do think that he favors them based on something in them.

They were good enough, or smart enough, or humble enough—they were *something* enough—to get plugged into the salvation system. But Calvinism says God truly "shows no partiality" even up to the very highest level. For all we don't know about the mystery of his selection of his people, we do know that he doesn't choose people based on anything they bring to the table. That would seem to place God's impartiality as high on the priority list as it's possible to go.

10) Doesn't Calvinism undermine evangelism?

If everyone's eternal fate is under God's control and can't be changed, why bother evangelizing? Won't all the elect come to salvation whether I bother to share the gospel with them or not?

I think this view is erroneous, but I know it will be tough to convince the critics—and that's not their fault; it's ours. Unfortunately, we Calvinists have given the critics some pretty strong grounds to support their case. In the last century, the churches most strongly associated with Calvinism—those in the Presbyterian, Reformed, and related traditions—have generally not been at the forefront of evangelistic efforts. We used to be; in earlier centuries, it was Calvinist churches that were most particularly known for doing a lot of evangelism. Lately, however, our abdication has left it to others to take the lead.

There have been exceptions, such as the enormous Evangelism Explosion ministry created by D. James Kennedy and Coral Ridge Presbyterian Church. But exceptions are what they were, and no one knew that better than they did. I attended Evangelism Explosion classes at Coral Ridge, which, in spite of his failing powers, Kennedy continued to teach personally right up to his death. I will never forget hearing him describe how he dealt with people who criticized his program's approach to evangelism. "I always ask them," he said, "how they do it differently in their evangelism programs. And it always turns out that they don't have any evangelism programs. So I tell them, 'I like the way I do it wrong better than the way you don't do it right.'"

However, I don't think it's Calvinism that has led these churches to neglect evangelism. I think the opposite. I think they've become less evangelistic because they've become less robustly Calvinist. For most of the history of Calvinism, Calvinist churches were the world's leaders in evangelism. In the last century or so, they haven't been. And what do you know? Right at the same time their evangelism was fading, they were losing their grip on the deep culture of Calvinism. "Calvinism" was becoming for them an ideology rather than a way of life. And in the absence of a deep culture to support it, even the ideology became shallow, centered not on the joy of resting in God's controlling all things to glorify himself by loving us, but on technical esoterica and negations. Nothing demonstrates this more than the sweeping intellectual conquest of the "five points." (That's the very last time I'll complain about the five points, I promise.)

Naturally, evangelistic leadership has passed to those who not only know what they believe, but have built church communities that intentionally embody their beliefs in all of life and in all activities of life. You can't (with all due respect to Kennedy) mobilize large numbers of believers to actively evangelize just by having "programs" for evangelism. You do it by sustaining a church culture centered on whole-life discipleship.[8]

In fact, real Calvinism doesn't undermine evangelism. Yes, the ultimate fate of each person is in God's control. But God is not capricious; he has a complete and integrated plan for all events, and absolutely everything that happens is part of the plan. That includes my decision to evangelize or not evangelize. So the ultimate fate of the unbelievers around me is not unrelated to my decision whether to evangelize them. (In a universe totally under God's control, no two facts are unrelated. All facts are related to one another as parts of God's plan.) God is capable of saving those people without my help, of course, but it may well be that his plan is for them to be saved because I chose to evangelize them—or be lost because I chose not to. As Kennedy dreadfully warned us in that evangelism class, "There are people out there who will go to hell unless you share the gospel with them."

Real Calvinism actually provides invaluable encouragement to evangelism. How else can we be sure that our efforts are not in vain? Without Calvinism, the success of our efforts is ultimately in the hands of the unbelievers we evangelize. With Calvinism, our ultimate success is in God's hands. Like most Christians, I'm not called to go into dangerous and forbidding mission fields to preach the gospel. But if I were, I know that the only way I could possibly do so with confidence would be because I believe the Holy Spirit takes the occasion of our evangelism to work a supernatural transformation that can convert absolutely anyone.

11) Doesn't Calvinism say you can be absolutely sure you're saved? Isn't that arrogant?

One of the distinctive teachings of Calvinism (and Lutheranism) is that God's people should know for sure that they are saved—not only that they are saved right now, but that they are saved forever and will be in heaven for eternity. To the Calvinist (or Lutheran), "being saved" implies all this; we cannot separate our present right standing with God from our future enjoyment of heaven because the one follows from the other. Arminianism teaches that you can know for sure you are right with God at the present moment and would go to heaven if you died right now. But you could lose your salvation in the future by turning away from God, and therefore you can't know for sure that you will go to heaven if you don't die right now. In other words, you can know for sure that you "are saved" but not that you "will be saved." The Roman church rejects both positions and pronounces an anathema on anyone who holds them. Rome says no one can be sure of his or her right standing with God even at a given moment.

Those who reject the Calvinist/Lutheran view often say that it's arrogant to think we can know for sure we are saved and will never turn away from God. The Bible does warn us, very clearly and with a terrifying sternness, that some people think they're saved when they're not. "There are those who are clean in their own eyes but are not washed of their filth" (Prov. 30:12). This unspeakably evil presumption on God's grace has its root in the self-deception of the human heart. "The heart is deceitful above all things, and desperately sick; who can understand it?" (Jer. 17:9). Nothing is more commonplace than for people to deceive themselves, and the subject people are most often self-deceived about is themselves—their own hearts and lives.

The Bible therefore admonishes us to examine ourselves and find out whether our faith is genuine. "Be all the more diligent to make your calling and election sure" (2 Pet. 1:10). "We desire each one of you to show the same earnestness to have the full assurance of hope until the end" (Heb. 6:11).

This raises an urgent question: How can we ever possibly know that we're not self-deceived? We can't step outside our own heads and hearts to look at them objectively. If we recognize that we're sinners with self-deceptive hearts, wouldn't it be arrogant to think that we could ever be really sure we had a true faith?

That sounds very plausible. And my own natural inclinations are all in that direction. I've actually lived through the experience of having a false certainty of my salvation. I had what can only be described as a demonically wicked presumption toward God and self-deception toward myself. So I know firsthand how easy it is to have a false faith and think that it's true. If the Bible taught that you could never be sure of your salvation, that would seem like the most natural thing in the world to me.

However, I'm afraid the Bible completely forecloses that option. It insists that God's people can and should know for sure that they are God's people. This is not something that appears just in a few isolated texts. The Bible is saturated with it. Every page of the Bible takes it for granted that believers are both able to know and obligated to know—for sure—that they are saved. (If you're looking for a few texts to start with in examining what the Bible says about this, check out 2 Tim. 1:12; Heb. 6:11–12; 2 Pet. 1:3–11; and 1 John 3:14; 5:13.)

There are three ways uncertainty about our salvation can arise. First, you may be uncertain about whether Christianity is true. But this book is for believers, so I'll leave that whole subject aside.

Second, you may hold a theology which denies that everyone who has true faith is saved. Obviously if we have to contribute something beyond faith, we can't be sure whether our contribution is good enough to accomplish our salvation. So if you are not absolutely clear that salvation is by faith apart from the works of the law—or, worse, if you positively deny this truth—then obviously you can have no certainty of salvation. Any reliance on the works of the law, to any extent, destroys assurance.

Unfortunately, Calvin often wrote as though those two ways were the only two ways people might doubt their own salvation. When he encountered believers who doubted their salvation, he usually assumed that the problem must be a lack of full understanding and full acceptance of the doctrine of salvation through faith alone. And, alas, much of the Calvinist tradition has imbibed this error from Calvin.

But there is a third way to doubt your salvation. You may believe that everyone with true faith is saved, but you may doubt whether your own faith is a true and living faith. James warns us dreadfully that some people have "dead" faith (James 2:14–26). How can I know whether my faith is a living, saving faith? This is the problem of subjectivity. How can I ever examine whether I'm self-deceived, when I'm the one who's doing the examining?

This problem of self-deception is of course a challenge for all Christians, but many people think it is especially acute in the case of Calvinism. Every other theological tradition says that we contribute something to the process of appropriating salvation— we do something that gets us plugged into the salvation system. We make a decision to believe, or we use the sacraments, or we do something else. People cling to those actions as the answer to self-deception. I made a decision to believe, so I know that I really believe. But the Calvinistic understanding says that we contribute nothing as we come to faith. If we do nothing, how can we know our faith is true?

I think people are mistaken when they say this is more of a challenge for Calvinism than for anybody else. It seems obvious to me that many people are self-deceived when they "make a decision for Christ" or use the sacraments. Certainly many people experience anxiety about whether their "decisions for Christ" were genuine. And it's not like Calvinism denies that there's a subjective experience that believers participate in as they come to faith! The human will responds to the work of the Spirit.

However, that still leaves us with the original problem. How can we know we're not self-deceived?

The biblical answer to the problem is to examine our lives. Living faith will always, infallibly, produce an effect on our outward behavior. The entire book of 1 John is about this, from beginning to end. John explicitly tells us that this is the purpose of the letter: "I write these things to you who believe in the name of the Son of God that you may know that you have eternal life" (1 John 5:13). Throughout the letter, John insists that assurance is grounded in the evidence of faith provided by godly works: "By this we know that we have come to know him, if we keep his commandments" (1 John 2:3). We also find the same principle in other passages like James 2:14–26 and 2 Peter 1:3–11. Looking to our behavior to confirm that our faith is real faith is not works-righteousness. It is, instead, acknowledging the role that works really do play in the Christian life.

Even Calvin sometimes overcame his muddle-headedness about this issue. Commenting on 1 John 2:3 ("And by this we know that we have come to know him, if we keep his commandments") he writes:

We are not hence to conclude that faith depends on works; for though every one receives a testimony to his faith from his works, yet it does not follow that it is founded on them, since they are added as an evidence. Then the certainty of faith depends on the grace of Christ alone, but piety and holiness of life distinguish true faith from that knowledge of God which is fictitious and dead; for the truth is, that those who are in Christ, as Paul says, have put off the old man.[9]

And at least some writers in the Calvinist tradition have more fully and systematically overcome Calvin's error. The best thing ever written about assurance may well be chapter 11 of Arthur Pink's masterpiece *Studies on Saving Faith*:

> God himself has supplied us with tests, and we are mad if we do not avail ourselves of them. . . . The Holy Spirit himself moved one of his servants to write a whole epistle to instruct us how we might know whether or not we have eternal life. Does that look as though the question may be determined and settled as easily as so many present-day preachers and writers represent it? If nothing more than a firm persuasion of the truth of John 3:16 or 5:24 be needed to assure me of my salvation, then why did God give a whole epistle to instruct us on this subject?[10]

Contrary to what people often assume, certainty does not have to mean arrogance. Hitler was absolutely, unshakably sure that his barbaric master-race religion was right. But the people who fought against him were just as absolutely, unshakably sure that it was wrong. And they were absolutely, unshakably sure that they were right to fight against Hitler. Their absolute certainty of the righteousness of their cause was the only thing that saw them through all the dark times—the times when it looked as though Hitler would win. If they'd had the slightest doubt, they'd have caved a dozen times. But they stood strong to the end because they were absolutely sure. Was that arrogant?

In fact, arrogance and humility are a great test of assurance. The false assurance of wicked people who presume on God's grace always produces an insufferable arrogance. But the true assurance of God's people who really possess his promises always produces humility. As A. A. Hodge puts it:

I think the first essential mark of the difference between true and false assurance is to be found in the fact that the true works humility. There is nothing in the world that works such satanic, profound, God-defiant pride as false assurance; nothing works such utter humility, or brings to such utter self-emptiness, as the child-like spirit of true assurance.[11]

12) What about the passage where it says . . ?

In this book, while I have tried to point to some of the scriptural support for the Calvinist position, I have not engaged in detailed analysis of Scripture. In particular, I haven't gone over the scriptural passages that are typically cited against Calvinism and explained what I think about them. I'm not even going to do it here in the appendix. This may strike you as strange, or even dishonest. But before you write me off, let me explain why I have chosen this approach.

This whole book has really been wrestling with a paradox that lies right at the heart of theology. Obviously the whole point of theology is to understand what the Bible says. In one sense, then, theology is all about interpreting passages of Scripture. Yet if Scripture is the Word of God—and we wouldn't be interested in it if we didn't believe it is—then all of it must be true. So when we seek to understand each Bible passage, we have to bring to it our understanding of the total biblical witness. And yet, what is the total biblical witness but the accumulation of our understanding of all the individual Bible passages? Systematic theology is based on Bible interpretation, and Bible interpretation is based on systematic theology. Which comes first, the chicken or the egg?

In other words, when we do theology we are always thinking about two things. One is a coherent, integrated theological witness that we believe Scripture as a whole constitutes. The other is the separate meanings of all the individual Scripture passages. Neither one of these can be totally subordinated to the other. You can't do without the coherent, integrated system because you need that system to guide you as you read the individual passages. And you can't do without the individual passages because you need them to guide you as you study the system.

This is simply the way the human mind works. All knowledge, not just theology, involves some form of this problem. That's why epistemology and semiotics are such difficult fields!

Calvinistic writers have done a great job of handling the disputes over particular passages of Scripture. If you read up on, say, the controversy over how to interpret Romans 7, you will find Calvinists laying out a good argument for why that passage is consistent with Calvinism. There is really nothing new that I can contribute to those kinds of arguments. The scholars, the real experts, have those bases covered already. If I tried to do it with my inferior knowledge, I'd just foul it all up.

I wrote this book because most people, when they first approach the question of whether Calvinism is true, aren't yet ready to delve into that kind of argument. First they need to learn what Calvinism is. You can't very well evaluate the argument over whether Romans 7 supports or refutes Calvinism until you understand what the word "Calvinism" means. And today most people just have no idea at all what Calvinism is—for all the reasons I laid out back in the introduction and the Detour.

That's what I've been after in this book. My job has been to put you in a position where you can give the particular scriptural arguments for Calvinism (and, for that matter, the scriptural arguments against Calvinism) a fair hearing. If you read this book and then put it down wanting to ask me, "Okay, now I understand why some people find Calvinism so plausible, but what about the passage where it says . . . ?" then I've done my job and can now turn you over to the real experts for further treatment.

Notes

Introduction

1. The exact history of "the five points" and TULIP is messy—see the appendix, question 2, for more information.

2. In drawing this analogy between the way we talk about Calvinism and the way we talk about the incarnation, I am not trying to suggest that Calvinism is essential to Christianity, as the incarnation is, such that anyone who rejects it is outside the faith and not (yet) saved!

Detour

1. "Westminster Confession of Faith," Orthodox Presbyterian Church, accessed August 17, 2011, http://www.opc.org/wcf.html.

2. R. C. Sproul remarks that section 3.1 of the Confession is not even particularly Calvinist. The assertion that God ordains everything that comes to pass is simply theism; all Christian theological traditions agree on this. The differences arise when we confront subsequent questions like the relationship between God's ordaining of events and his foreknowledge of them. See R. C. Sproul, *Chosen by God* (Carol Stream, IL: Tyndale, 1986), 25–28.

3. See especially book 2, chapter 2, section 7, the same point is strongly affirmed at the end of section 5 and at the beginning and end of section 8.

4. Stephen Wilson, *Virtue Reformed: Rereading Jonathan Edwards's Ethics* (Leiden, Netherlands: Koninklijke Brill, 2005), 59; see also Perry Miller, "Preparation for Salvation in Seventeenth-Century New England," *Journal of the History of Ideas* (June 1943): 261.

5. John Calvin, *Institutes of the Christian Religion*, book 2, chapter 3, section 3, trans. Ford Battles (Louisville, KY: Westminster John Knox Press, 2006), 292. Numerous other examples from the *Institutes* and Calvin's other writings could be presented on this point. This is not just something Calvin said once; it runs through his whole theology. See also the Westminster Confession's carefully crafted, precisely worded statements at WCF 16.7, which also affirm this view.

6. For example, it portrays the giving of the moral law to humanity as a free, unmerited blessing (see WCF 7.1 and 7.2).

7. See for example WCF 3.7 and 5.4.

8. Sproul, *Chosen*, p. 96.

9. B. B. Warfield, "The Plan of Salvation," *Monergism*, accessed August 12, 2011, http://www.monergism.com/thethreshold/articles/onsite/WarfieldPlan_index.html.

10. "It is probable . . . that Calvin's greatest contribution to theological science lies in the rich development which he gives—and which he was the first to give—to the doctrine of the work of the Holy Spirit." B. B. Warfield "John Calvin the Theologian," *ReformationINK*, accessed August 17, 2011, http://homepage.mac.com/shanerosenthal/reformationink/bbwcalvin1.htm.

11. See WCF 2.3.

12. B. B. Warfield, "The Theology of John Calvin," *ReformationINK*, accessed August 17, 2011, http://homepage.mac.com/shanerosenthal/reformationink/bbwcalvin2.htm.

Chapter 2: God Loves You Unconditionally

1. C. S. Lewis, *The Four Loves*, in *The Inspirational Writings of C.S. Lewis*, (New York: Inspirational, 1994), 279–80.

2. If you're not comfortable with my use of the term "nature," you can substitute "the general system of the creation order" and nothing important in my argument will change. What's really important to my argument here is not the distinction between the natural and the supernatural, but between God and creation (which includes both nature and created supernatural beings). I happen to think that human free will is part of "nature" as we usually

use that term, but I don't ultimately need to rely on that premise; what I really rely on here is the premise that the human will is a part of the created order and is therefore subordinate to God's creative activity.

3. This may not appear to be strictly accurate given that Rome allows for salvation outside the ordinary working of the sacraments, through such things as a desire for baptism that gets thwarted by other events, or the receipt of excess merits built up by works of supererogation. But this is an illusion. Forming a desire for baptism or receiving supererogatory merits is just another way of getting plugged into the sacramental system, and what determines whether you get plugged in is the unfolding of nature rather than God's independent choice.

4. "God gave them free will: thus surrendering a portion of his omnipotence." C. S. Lewis, *Miracles*, in *The Complete C.S. Lewis Signature Classics*, (New York: HarperCollins, 2002), 277.

5. Personally, I'm inclined to think that God's treatment of the lost is not only good, but it's even good *for them*. We are moral agents, and we are better off being held responsible for our sins than being treated like mere animals whose choices don't matter. In some ways it's just as much a sign of his amazing love for us that he cares enough to hold us accountable as that he also pardons some of us. Speaking as a person who definitely deserves infinite and eternal suffering, I'm not sure I would have taken it as a sign of love if God had told me he would let me off the hook simply because he couldn't be bothered to do anything about my depravity. But while God's treatment of the lost may be for their good, it is clearly not for their highest and fullest good.

6. B. B. Warfield, "The Plan of Salvation," *Monergism*, accessed August 17, 2011, http://www.monergism.com/thethreshold/articles/onsite/WarfieldPlan_index.html.

Chapter 3: God Loves You Irresistibly

1. The idea of faith producing blessing in our lives inevitably raises the specter of the prosperity gospel. Let me emphasize that the problems I'm referring to here are problems I've observed in otherwise sound gospel preaching. This is a completely different issue from dealing with the horde of religious hucksters and con artists who have figured out how to make big bucks as spiritual parasites in the body of Christ. There is a very clear line between, on the one hand, sound gospel preaching that is weakened (in my opinion) by the influence of the Spirit-as-persuader model, and, on the other hand, preaching that is based upon false promises that negate everything the Bible tells us about the Christian life. One of America's most prominent "preachers"—I hesitate to call him that because I'm not sure he's ever actually preached the gospel—promises in one of his nationally bestselling books that if you're a true believer, the checkout line in the grocery store will go faster for you. (If he really thinks so, why isn't his church taking advantage of this? He should have evangelists going to the store and offering to wait in line with people, so they can experience the transforming power of Jesus for themselves!) But God forbid I should hold my Arminian brothers and sisters responsible for *that* sort of thing. In some ways, it's a testimony to their ministry that the con artists choose to emulate them. There was a time when religious con artists tried to pass themselves off as Presbyterians; that they no longer do so is not a positive testimony for the ministry of Presbyterian churches.

2. I use the words "miracle" and "miraculous" in their popular sense rather than their technical theological sense. Theologians would not call the work of the Holy Spirit in our hearts "miraculous" because they use the term "miracle" to refer only to outward manifestations of God's power over nature. I use the term in the popular sense, to mean any exertion of God's power to alter the usual course of nature, whether it is outwardly manifested or not.

3. John Calvin, *Commentary upon the Acts of the Apostles*, trans. Christopher Featherstone, 1585, commentary on Acts 2:21, http://www.ccel.org/ccel/calvin/calcom36. I have updated some archaic words in the translation.

Chapter 4: God Loves You Unbreakably

1. C. S. Lewis, *The Four Loves*, in *The Inspirational Writings of C. S. Lewis*, (New York: Inspirational, 1994), 278–79.

2. In the nineteenth century, an absurd idea began circulating that Calvin and/or Calvinists think material prosperity is a sign of divine favor. The original source of this idea was Max Weber, who hated Calvinists with a vicious passion and did not scruple to write all sorts of outrageously false propaganda against them. For example, Weber points to the scene in *The Pilgrim's Progress* where Christian is willing to follow God even though his wife

Notes

and children refuse, and says that it shows us how much Calvinists hate their families. "The Calvinist's intercourse with his God was carried on in deep spiritual isolation," Weber writes. "Wife and children cling to him, but stopping his ears with his fingers and crying, 'life, eternal life,' he staggers forth across the fields. No refinement could surpass the naïve feeling of the tinker who, writing in his prison cell, earned the applause of a believing world in expressing the emotions of a faithful Puritan, thinking only of his own salvation. . . . Only when he himself is safe does it occur to him that it would be nice to have his family with him" (Max Weber, *The Protestant Ethic and the Spirit of Capitalism* (New York: Charles Scribner's Sons, 1958), 106. Anyone who has read *The Pilgrim's Progress* in an unbiased spirit will see what a reckless and even savage hatred must be involved in producing such an irresponsible misrepresentation. Weber's assertion that Calvinists take prosperity as a sign of divine favor is equally groundless. Alas, following the usual method of scholarly progress, what began as vicious calumny became a daring and innovative thesis, then a rising intellectual movement, then the predominant academic view, then conventional wisdom, then a fact so deeply accepted that for a long time few even thought to question it anymore. The orderly processes of objective scholarship were not hindered by the mere fact of the claim being preposterously contrary to the facts, which anyone can find by simply opening the relevant books and reading them. (Thank goodness nothing like that ever happens in the academy today!) In fact, Calvin insisted that we shouldn't measure divine favor by anyone's material circumstances, but if we did, it would be poverty, deprivation, and other forms of suffering that would indicate divine favor, because God does not promise prosperity to believers, but he does promise to use suffering to sanctify them (see especially his comments on Isaiah 36:10 in his Scripture commentaries, and also in *Institutes of the Christian Religion*, book II, chapter 10, sections 10–21, where he argues at length that the heroes of the Old Testament's willingness to endure poverty and affliction proves that their hope was in a future life). This may help explain why it was especially the rich and powerful of Geneva who hated Calvin and schemed relentlessly to undermine and destroy him throughout his career; the wealthy Genevans' desire to enjoy the respectability of church membership while living grossly immoral lives was always the primary obstacle to Calvin's reformational efforts (see Derek Thomas, "Who Was John Calvin?" and D. G. Hart, "The Reformer of Faith and Life," in *John Calvin: A Heart for Devotion, Doctrine and Doxology*, ed. Buck Parsons, (Sanford, FL: Reformation Trust, 2008).

3. John Calvin, *Commentaries on the Epistles of Paul to the Philippians, Colossians and Thessalonians*, trans. John Pringle, 1851, commentary on Philippians 4:4, http://www.ccel.org/ccel/calvin/calcom42.html. I have updated some archaic words in the translation.

4. John Calvin, *Commentaries on the Catholic Epistles*, trans. John Owen, 1855, commentary on James 1:2. http://www.ccel.org/ccel/calvin/calcom45.html. I have updated some archaic words in the translation.

5. John Calvin, *Letters of John Calvin*, ed. Jules Bonnet, trans. M. R. Gilbert, vol. IV (Philadelphia: PA, Presbyterian Board of Education, 1858), 320–21.

6. This point is especially important because many people reject Calvinism on grounds that if we play no role in our salvation, we have no way to distinguish true faith from false; see the appendix, question 11.

7. You could also change the order if you wanted, putting the Father's election first, with the work of the Son and the Spirit following. That would represent the chronological order and, so to speak, the causal chain of the work of salvation. The order I follow here is epistemological or experiential—the Christian comes to know first that Jesus saves him, then goes on to deduce from this that the Father chose him and the Spirit regenerated him.

8. "Christians can and should be assured of their eternal election. This is evident from the fact that Scripture addresses them as the chosen ones and comforts them with their election (Eph. 1:4; 2 Thess. 2:13)." "A Brief Statement of the Doctrinal Position of the Missouri Synod," section 40, http://www.lcms.org/Document.fdoc?src=lcm&id=958.

9. Of course, there are many other things besides a lack of assurance that cause believers to experience less joy; and there are many other things besides rejection of the doctrine of the perseverance of the saints that cause believers to lack assurance (see the appendix, question 11).

10. Michael Novak, *No One Sees God: The Dark Night of Atheists and Believers* (New York: Doubleday, 2008), 92–93.

11. Novak, *No One*, 90.

Notes

Conclusion: The Joy of Calvinism

1. B. B. Warfield, "The Theology of John Calvin," *ReformationINK*, accessed August 18, 2011, http://homepage.mac.com/shanerosenthal/reformationink/bbwcalvin2.htm.

2. B. B. Warfield, "Some Thoughts Concerning Predestination," *The Christian Workers Magazine*, December 1916.

3. "For of Calvinism there is really only *one* point to be made in the field of soteriology: the point that *God saves sinners*." J. I. Packer, "A Quest for Godliness: The Puritan Vision of the Christian Life," introduction to *The Death of Death in the Death of Christ* by John Owen, Banner of Truth, 1958, http://www.monergism.com/thethreshold/articles/onsite/packer_intro.html.

4. C. S. Lewis, *Reflections on the Psalms* (San Diego, CA: Harcourt, Brace & World, 1958), 96–97.

Appendix: Questions and Answers

1. John Calvin, *Commentary on the Book of Psalms*, trans. James Anderson (Grand Rapids, MI: Baker, 2003), xli.

2. At least, in Switzerland this was what Reformation pastors expected. In other parts of Europe, Reformation pastors didn't always maintain such integrity. The standard set in nearby Zurich, where the Reformation did not need to compromise with immoral elites in order to survive, was probably a factor here.

3. John Calvin, *Letters of John Calvin*, vol. 1, ed. Jules Bonnet, trans. M. R. Gilbert (Philadelphia, PA: Presbyterian Board of Education, 1858), 344.

4. Calvin, *Letters*, vol. 2, 217.

5. "There is no historical association between the acrostic TULIP and the Canons of Dort." Richard Muller, "Was Calvin a Calvinist? Or, Did Calvin (or Anyone Else in the Early Modern Era) Plant the 'TULIP'?" 2009 Fall Lecture at the H. Henry Meeter Center for Calvin Studies, October 15, 2009, http://www.calvin.edu/meeter/lectures/Was%20Calvin%20 a%20Calvinist-12-26-09.pdf.

6. See Kenneth Stewart, "The Points of Calvinism: Retrospect and Prospect," *Scottish Bulletin of Evangelical Theology*, Autumn 2008, p. 187–203, http://www.covenant.edu/docs/ faculty/Stewart_Ken/Points%20of%20Calvinism%20Retrospect%20and%20Prospect.pdf and Kenneth Stewart, *Ten Myths about Calvinism*, [Downers Grove, IL: InterVarsity, 2011]). The first known reference to TULIP in print is reproduced in William Vail, "The Five Points of Calvinism Historically Considered," *The New Outlook*, 104 (May–August 1913): the article can be viewed through Google Books. It is unfortunate that Vail, in his diligent efforts to discover what the "five points" agreed on at Dort really were, consulted numerous authorities but failed to consult the actual canons of Dort. Had he done so, we might have been spared no end of trouble!

7. WCF 5.4.

8. Unfortunately there is no space here to get into the very complicated question of why Calvinist churches lost the deep culture of Calvinism and whole-life discipleship. For those who follow such questions, I can briefly indicate my position by saying that I think it's mainly because we've lost our understanding of common grace and the rich purposes of God's providential work in the world outside the church walls. Under such conditions, theology becomes scholastic and esoteric; ecclesiology becomes very "high church" and even quasi-Roman; discipleship becomes focused on doing religious works, rather than on the 98 percent of life that is not religious works; and our engagement with the world and its culture is either cut off entirely or delegated to a small priesthood class of professional do-gooders. (As D. R. Myddelton has wisely observed, the do-gooders really ought to be called "mean-wellers" because they mean well but rarely do much good.)

9. John Calvin, *Commentaries on the Catholic Epistles*, trans. John Owen, 1855, commentary on 1 John 2:3, http://www.ccel.org/ccel/calvin/calcom45.html. I have updated some archaic words in the translation.

10. Arthur Pink, *Studies on Saving Faith*, Reformed Church Publications, 2009, http:// www.pbministries.org/books/pink/Saving_Faith/saving_faith_11.htm.

11. A. A. Hodge, "Assurance and Humility," *oChristian.com*, accessed August 17, 2011, http://articles.ochristian.com/preacher261-1.shtml.

General Index

addiction, 34
Anabaptist tradition, 164
Arminian tradition, 54, 81, 94, 137, 187
assurance, 27–28, 44, 138, 190–95
Athanasian Creed, 17–18
atonement, 23–24, 54–62, 65–67, 107, 168
Augustine, 41–42, 148–49

baptism, 54, 56
blessing, 79–80, 86
Boettner, Lorraine, 166
Boice, James, 156
Bucer, Martin, 159

Calvin, Idelette de Bure, 161–62
Calvin, John, 16, 31–32, 37, 128–29, 149, 157–64, 169–71, 193–94
Canons of Dort, 39–40
Charles V, 160
children, 116–19
choice, 97–99, 112–13
Christian ethics, 72–74
church discipline, 160–61
church membership, 160
commandments, 13
communication, 13–14
conversion, 33, 99, 102
covenants, 99

discipleship, 59, 200

Edwards, Jonathan, 20, 35
election, 42, 61, 165–66
emotions, 13, 47–48, 145–48
Engle, Jim, 145
Erasmus, 31, 171
evangelism, 97, 188–90
evil, 38, 185

faith, 42, 54, 64, 97, 128, 131, 137–40, 192–95, 198
Fall, 180–83
Farel, Guillaume, 160–62
fear, 138–39, 150–52

Five Points (of Calvinism), 15–16, 29–45, 164–67
"four-point" Calvinism, 168–71
Francis I, 157–60
free will, 20, 23, 30–33, 39, 80, 135–36, 149, 171–77
freedom, 33–34

Geneva Bible, 164
God
    efficacious power of, 248–50
    glory of, 77, 79, 116
    hate of, 93
    image of, 25, 36, 78, 126
    incomprehensibility of, 22–23
    irresistible love of, 92–119
    kingdom of, 71
    love as unbreakable, 130–43
    omnipotence of, 172–74
    personal love of, 39–40, 48–53, 63–67
    sovereignty of, 40–44, 82–83
    unconditional love of, 69–90
    will of, 184–85
good works, 54
goodness, 37–39, 76–78, 90
grace, 41, 152–54

hell, 152
Hodge, A. A., 194–95
holiness, 133, 152–54
Holy Spirit, 33–35, 42 43, 59, 74, 93–119, 133–35, 175–76
Horton, Michael, 156
human nature, 79, 94–95
hyper-Calvinism, 40

ignorance, 22–25
impartiality, 184–88

Jesus
    divinity of, 17–18
    lordship of, 98
    personal love of, 49–52

General Index

substitutionary atonement of, 53–62, 65–67, 107, 168–69
joy, 17, 125–26, 130–48
judgment, 40, 59, 186–87
justice, 85–86, 90

Kennedy, D. James, 188–90
knowledge, 23–24

law, 151
law of noncontradiction, 172–73
legalism, 133
Lewis, C. S., 72, 83, 124, 154
Lord's Supper, 54
Luther, Martin, 31, 41, 157, 171
Lutheran tradition, 54, 80–81, 137–38, 164

marriage, 71–73, 108–12
means of grace, 54–57, 80–81
mercy, 86
miracle, 198
misunderstandings of Calvinism, 15–21, 29
moral inability, 177–80
moral law, 106–8
moral responsibility, 31–33, 79
Mouw, Richard, 156

nature, 79–85, 197
new birth, 175–76
new creation, 100–105, 115–16, 123
Novak, Michael, 141–43

obedience, 14, 59, 151–52
original sin, 23, 37–38, 81, 95, 180

Parsons, Burk, 156
Pelagianism, 41, 180
Pelagius, 148
persecution, 163–64
perseverance, 128–38
persuasion, 95–96, 104, 112, 116
Peterson, Robert, 156
Pink, Arthur, 194
preaching, 94–96, 101, 198
predestination, 40–44
providence, 23, 30, 33, 168–72

reconciliation, 113–14
Reformation, 157–64
regeneration, 33, 36, 42, 135
repentance, 95, 101, 131, 184–85
resurrection, 126–27
righteousness, 107

Roman tradition, 53–54, 62, 80, 94, 107, 137, 141, 159–64, 190
Ryken, Philip, 156

sacraments, 62, 80, 94, 192–93, 198
salvation, 15–16, 25–28, 41, 50–62, 81–82, 132–33, 137, 153, 183–88
sanctification, 123, 132–33, 140
Satan, 31–32, 39
self-deception, 191–93
self-righteousness, 133
sin, 31–32, 36, 56–57, 59, 85, 89–90, 99–101, 104, 131, 171, 177–80
soteriology, 15
spiritual priorities, 71–76
Sproul, R. C., 40, 156
Steele, David, 166
suffering, 123–43
Synod of Dort, 165–66
systematic theology, 21–23, 195–96

Thomas, Curtis, 166
totally depravity, 35–39, 165–67
transformation, 101–6, 115
Trinity, 43, 100
TULIP. *see* Five Points (of Calvinism)

visible church, 54

Warfield, B. B., 43, 89–90, 149–50
Weber, Max, 198–99
Westminster Catechism, 154
Westminster Confession of Faith, 29–30, 33, 37–39, 44, 174–77
will, 104, 108, 111, 115, 137. *see also* free will; God, will of
Williams, Michael, 156
worship, 62–63, 152
wrath, 55, 58, 151

Scripture Index

Genesis

1	37, 107
3:9	93
4:4–5	185
9:6	36
18:27–33	23
22:2	122
22:12	122
50:20	23

Exodus

34:7	23, 106

Leviticus

11:44	123
22:32	123

Numbers

14:18	23

Deuteronomy

10:15	64
29:29	87

2 Samuel

12:22–23	117
22:51	64

Job

7:17–18	74

Psalms

8:4–6	74
22:9	117
51:8	131
51:10	176
51:12	131
82:6	34

Proverbs

16:4	89
17:3	133
30:12	191

Isaiah

1:25	133
46:9–10	88
48:11	76–77
53:5	55
55:10–11	101

Jeremiah

17:9	191

Ezekiel

11:19	105, 176
18	23
33:11	113, 183
36:26	105, 176

Daniel

4:35	86

Nahum

1:3	23

Malachi

1:2–3	72

Matthew

1:21	60
5:28	73, 104
5:43–48	86
5:44–45	123
6:33	71
7:7–8	113
9:15	98
10:29–31	23, 86
11:19	98

11:20–24	89	10:34–35	187
19:13–15	117	10:47	59
19:25–26	178		
21:16	117	**Romans**	
23:23	36	1–2	24
23:25–26	73	2	187
23:37	93	2:11	185, 187
26:24	89	2:14	36
26:53–54	76, 179	2:15	37
		3:10–18	113
Mark		5:3	14, 125
7:21	104	5:9	59
10:13–16	117	5:19	60
10:18	37	7	196
16:7	132	8:14–17	109
		8:15	98
Luke		8:22	77
1:41–44	117	8:28	76–77
7:34	98	8:32	74
7:50	59	8:38–39	78
14:26	72	8:39	77
18:15–17	117	9:1–29	89
18:19	138	9:13	186
		9:19–23	23
John		12:2	176
1:12	186		
3:3	178	**1 Corinthians**	
3:8	101	1:18	59
3:16	75	1:26–31	186–87
3:19–20	93	3:6	96, 98
3:27	178	4:15–16	7
6:44	35	5:5	59
6:60	100	7:22	171
6:63	100	7:32–34	71
6:65	100	9:24	59
8:24	59	13:8	125
10:34–36	34	15:3	126
13:1	65	15:14	126
15:5	178		
15:9	65	**2 Corinthians**	
15:12	65	3:18	59
15:13	65	4:16	176
17:23	65	5:17	105
18:11	76	5:21	24, 55, 107
19:26	186		
20:28	17	**Galatians**	
21:15–19	132	1:3–4	60
		6:15	105
Acts			
10:34	185		

Scripture Index

Ephesians

1:3–4	59
1:3–10	65
1:3–14	87
2:5	105
2:8	59
4:23	176
5:25	71

Philippians

2:6–7	74–75
2:12	59
4:4	13, 128
4:4–7	139

Colossians

1:16–17	138
2:13	105
2:23	63
3:10	176

1 Thessalonians

5:8	59
5:9	23
5:16–18	14, 126

2 Thessalonians

1:8	98
2:7	139

1 Timothy

1:15	85
5:8	72
6:17	84

2 Timothy

1:9	59
1:12	192
2:13	138, 172, 179
3:16–17	101

Titus

3:5	59, 176

Hebrews

6:11	191
6:11–12	192

James

1:2	129
1:2–4	128
1:12	128
2:14–26	192–93

1 Peter

1:3–5	131
1:3–7	18–19
1:5	59
1:6–7	131
2:8	23, 89
2:24	24, 55, 107
4:11	101
4:17	98

2 Peter

1:1–11	28
1:3–11	192–93
1:10	191

1 John

1:5	11
1:6	59, 93
1:9	28
2:3	193–94
3:1	186
3:1–2	109
3:14	192
4:7–12	64
4:10	60
4:18	139
5:13	192–93

Jude

4	89

Revelation

19:6–10	111
21:5	105
22:15	93